Spo

'The emperor's Summer Palace taken and sacked affording immense spoil. Emperor fled to Tartary.' A message sent back to London by Lord Elgin, the British High Commissioner to China, in 1860 during the final stages of the Second Opium War.

By Andrew Shaw

Mobius Publishing

Book design by Andrew Shaw
Cover design by Andrew Shaw
ISBN - Paperback: 9798871176184

To Holly.

CONTENTS

Introduction

Glossary

Bibliography

End Notes

Introduction

This book argues that all treasures looted from China by the West should be returned. There are no moral or ethical reasons for museums, other institutions, or collectors to hold on to these items. They were taken, often at gunpoint and with considerable loss of life, from a country unable to resist rapacious Western nations.

The British began the looting during the First Opium War (1839-42). The French were with them for the Second Opium War (1856-60). Soldiers from Germany, Italy, the Austro-Hungarian Empire, Russia, Japan and the United States joined them during a third conflict in 1900. You can add to their ranks the sepoys of the British Indian regiments and a contingent of Australian soldiers who also plundered.

It wasn't just soldiers who looted. Diplomats and the correspondents sent to cover the wars were also guilty. By the end of the nineteenth century, even the missionaries sent to save heathen souls had joined in.

While the looting done by the Japanese was at least equal to that of the West, this book does not focus on them. Japan does get its own chapter but as a Westerner, I concentrate on the crimes committed by Western nations.

This book is not aimed at people who already support the

idea that what was taken should be returned. It is aimed at those who have not yet given this matter any serious consideration. It hopes to persuade them to add their voices to the growing demand for what was stolen to be given back.

It is a book that can be read in a day and tells a story that should not be forgotten. The facts are taken from the numerous memoirs of those who took part in the wars against China and the wealth of academic research on the subject. Most importantly, it offers a solution to a problem that continues to sour relations between China and the West.

Glossary

Amoy	Xiamen
Burma	Myanmar
Canton	Guangzhou
Chusan	Zhoushan
Cixi	Dowager Empress who effectively ruled China for nearly half a century until her death in 1908.
Daoguang	Emperor 1820 – 1850
Jiaqing	Emperor of China 1796 – 1820
Nanking	Nanjing
Peking	Beijing
Port Arthur	Lüshun
Puyi	Emperor of China 1908 – 1912
Qing Dynasty	The Qing dynasty was founded by the Manchus who conquered China in 1644. It was the last imperial dynasty. Puyi was its last emperor. It collapsed in 1912. The invasions by foreign powers during the 19th century hastened its end.
Qianlong	Emperor of China 1735 – 1796
Xianfeng	Emperor of China 1850 – 1861
Xuantong	Emperor of China 1908 – 1912 (also known as Puyi)
Yuanmingyuan	The Summer Palace
Siam	Thailand
UNESCO Cultural	United Nations Educational, Scientific and Organization.

Camellia Sinensis, the tea plant.

1   An Unquenchable Thirst

It could be argued that the looting of China had its roots in the British passion for tea. It had been introduced to the court of King Charles the Second in the seventeenth century and soon became all the rage among the rich and powerful. It wasn't long before nearly everyone was drinking it.

There were those who disapproved. Jonas Hanway, an eighteenth century social reformer, was convinced it was bad for health. In 1767 he complained of a certain lane where beggars were often seen drinking it, as well as labourers mending roads enjoying it and tea in the cups of haymakers. As far as he was concerned it wasted time, lowered productivity and damaged the foreign trade balance.[1]

He was wrong in his belief that it was unhealthy. Drinking tea had the unintended impact of reducing mortality rates, as it led to more people boiling their water, which reduced their vulnerability to disease.[2] He had a point though, when it came to Britain's balance of payments. Thousands of tons of tea were being imported into Britain from China every year. As it poured in, silver poured out to pay for it, causing a huge trade deficit.

Britain tried to solve this problem by sending a diplomatic mission to Peking in the hope of persuading the Celestial Kingdom to buy British. It was led by Earl Macartney, who set off from Portsmouth on a blustery day in September 1792 in three ships laden with gifts for the emperor, Qianlong.

Macartney's brief was quite clear; it included negotiating the opening of new ports for trade, the establishment of a permanent embassy in Peking and the use of an island for British ships. The earl knew he faced an uphill task. The ruling Manchus, who'd conquered the vast Chinese nation a century and a half before and established the Qing dynasty, were highly suspicious of foreigners.

Merchants from Europe and America were restricted to thirteen factories on a strip of land on the outskirts of the southern port city of Canton. They had to buy tea and other goods through a few carefully selected merchants.

The first indication that Macartney might not succeed came soon after landing. A fleet of barges was provided for part of the journey from the coast to his audience with the emperor. Each barge was bedecked with pennants displaying Chinese characters. When the earl asked for their meaning, he was told they translated as 'barbarians bringing tribute to the emperor'. This was never going to be a meeting between equals to discuss trade. Macartney might have hoped he would negotiate on equal terms but the Manchus thought he'd come to offer homage to the Son of Heaven.

It is recorded in the annals of the Qing that on the tenth day of the eighth lunar month in the fifty eighth year of his reign, in a tent erected in the Garden of Ten Thousand Trees, in the imperial mountain retreat at Jehol, the Emperor Qianlong, Supreme Lord, Sacred Majesty, received an embassy and tribute from the king of the Western Ocean realm known as England.

It's remembered in English history books slightly differently. There it's written that on September 14th in the year of our Lord 1793 Earl Macartney, met the emperor of China and presented him with a letter from his sovereign, George III.

The earl had risen at 4 a.m. to dress himself in robes which he thought would dazzle Qianlong. He wore a suit of white velvet and a pink satin cloak lined with white taffeta. He boasted an enormous diamond broach at his breast and an ornamental frill of lace scattered with a sparkle of lesser diamonds. To all this, he added a chain of gold medallions weighing more than a kilo and, on his head, he placed a pink feathered hat.

Macartney and his delegation set off at dawn from their lodgings for their audience with the Lord of Ten Thousand Years. He and the other gentlemen of the expedition were preceded by an honour guard of British soldiers, dressed in their finest, marching to the beat of a military band playing God Save the King.

The solemnity of the occasion was marred somewhat by flocks of sheep and goats that often blocked the way and forced the procession into disarray. His lordship's dignity was ruffled further when he was stopped at the gates of the emperor's summer retreat to be told that all except the gentlemen of the expedition would have to wait outside. The earl was left kicking his heels for hours in a little side tent as the emperor enjoyed a leisurely breakfast in his private quarters.

Macartney hoped to be seen as an ambassador from an equally powerful and prosperous nation, so was not best pleased to learn that he wasn't the only embassy being received by the Dragon Throne that morning. He was lumped together with diplomats from Burma and the Kalmuck Mongols.

Nevertheless, he tried to make the best of it. When he was eventually summoned into the presence of Qianlong, he entered with all the gravitas he could muster, carrying a jewel encrusted golden casket above his head, containing the letter from His Majesty, King George III, which he placed with great ceremony into the hands of the emperor.

The earl had brought enough gifts with him to stock a small trade fair. They included telescopes, jewelled clocks, guns of every shape and size, musical instruments, Crown Derby porcelain, Wedgwood, portraits by Joshua Reynolds, two gilded carriages, a diving bell and even a hot air balloon. Qianlong was not impressed. The emperor fancied himself as something of a poet and had composed a verse for the occasion:

> Although they appear ordinary
> Their hearts are good and true
> Their gifts are not precious
> But no matter how meagre their offerings
> They have been treated generously.[3]

His imperial highness offered gifts in return. The earl and his deputy, Sir George Staunton, who was dressed in the scarlet robes of an Oxford Don, were given jade sceptres. Qianlong told them they were heirlooms that had been in his family for generations. The earl, a consummate diplomat, hid his disappointment. He later recalled that the one he received didn't appear to be of any great value.

His lack of appreciation only served to demonstrate his ignorance regarding the culture he was dealing with. To him, jade was no more than a pretty bauble. He was unaware that it was tradition for the emperor to offer gifts of at least equal worth in return for those he received as tribute. As far as Qianlong was concerned, a couple of antique jade sceptres, along with gifts of silver which he gave to each member of the British mission, were worth more than everything the earl had brought from England.

The emperor may not have thought much of Macartney's gifts but he was charmed by the earl's page boy, 12-year-old Tommy, the son of his deputy, Sir George. When told that the boy could speak to him without the need for an interpreter, he engaged him in a brief conversation. Qianlong was so delighted to find one so young had taken the time to learn his language that he rewarded him with a purse from his belt.

Once again, the significance of this was lost on the earl. The greatest honour the Son of Heaven could bestow on anybody was to offer something from his own person. The emperor seemed to attach far more importance to a young lad who could speak to him without the need for an interpreter than to Macartney and his many gifts.

While at Jehol, the earl tried to talk about trade with Qianlong's advisors but got nowhere. He and his party stuck around for a few days to enjoy the emperor's 83rd birthday celebrations. and were then ordered back to Peking. The mandarins surrounding the Son of Heaven were aware a few of Macartney's party suffered from the bloody flux as dysentery was known at the time and were keen to see the back of them.

The earl knew it was a problem. As many as eighteen members of his delegation lay bedridden in a makeshift hospital in the quarters they'd been given in the Chinese capital. When one of them died, hasty arrangements were made to hide the body.

By now, Macartney probably had a pretty good idea that his mission would not be successful. He continued to pester the emperor and his advisers but any lingering hopes he might have had were soon dispelled when he received a formal reply to his requests to expand trade. It was written in vermillion ink on imperial yellow silk: 'Our Celestial Empire possesses all things in prolific abundance,' the Son of Heaven informed the earl, 'and lacks no product within its borders. There is, therefore, no need to import the manufactures of outside barbarians in exchange for our own produce.'[4]

The earl and his party were told to leave. Earl Macartney, Viscount of Dervock, Baron of Lissanoure, Parkhurst and of Auchinleck, a friend of Edmund Burke, Dr. Samuel Johnson and Voltaire, had failed. According to his lordship's valet, Aeneas Anderson: 'We were received with the utmost politeness, treated with the utmost hospitality, watched with the utmost vigilance and dismissed with the utmost civility.'[5]

His lordship may not have got the trade concessions he wanted but he didn't leave empty handed. He and the rest of his party returned to their ships in Canton via the Grand Canal and Yangtse River. The journey through the heart of China allowed them to take notes on every aspect of the Qing Empire. In his arrogance, Qianlong wanted them to see the power and glory of his domain. He ordered regiment after regiment of his armies to line the shores of the rivers and canals as the flotilla of barges carrying the Earl and his men floated by.

This was a mistake. It was clear that the weaponry of the soldiers was positively medieval. Most were armed with spears, swords, and bows and arrows. Only a few had flintlocks and these were of ancient design. It was also noted that the navy protecting Chinese waters was next to useless.

Macartney wrote in his diary: 'that a couple of British frigates would be an overmatch for the whole naval force of the empire, that in half a summer they could destroy the entire navigation of their coasts' and that the armies could offer only feeble resistance.[6] He returned to London with this intelligence, which was filed away for future use.

Macartney's embassy was not the only attempt to get China to buy the abundance of British goods now pouring out of its factories. A little over twenty years later, Lord Amherst was sent to persuade Qianlong's successor, the Jiaqing Emperor, to buy British. He wasn't given the same courtesy as Macartney. Amherst didn't even get to meet the Son of Heaven. He was ordered out of Peking almost as soon as he arrived.

Queen Victoria as a young woman.

2 A Letter to Queen Victoria

Attempts to persuade China to open up for trade may have come to nothing but the British East India Company did discover a product that Chinese people craved – opium! [7]

At the time of the Macartney embassy in the 1790s, China imported about 200 tons from India every year. This was for medicinal purposes and the recreational use of the wealthy elite. By the late 1830s, ten times as much was being smuggled in. Like tea in Britain, opium began to be consumed at every level of society.

The Dragon Throne was aware of the dangers of the drug. Its importation and use were heavily regulated but the amount of money to be made was so great that there were plenty of traders willing to sell it to Chinese middlemen who then smuggled it into the Celestial Empire. The silver the foreign traders received was used to buy the tea and silk so popular back home. It helped ease Britain's trade deficit but at the same time, increasing numbers of Chinese people were becoming addicted.

China protested. The protests were ignored. A mandarin, Lin Zexu, was sent to Canton to deal with the problem. He wrote to Queen Victoria asking her to intervene: 'Where,' Lin wrote, 'is your conscience? I have heard that the smoking of opium is very strictly forbidden by your country ... then even less should you let it be passed on to the harm of other nations ...much less to China.'[8]

The letter was given into the care of Captain Warner of the cargo ship, the Thomas Coutts, who took it to London. He tried to make an appointment to see someone at the Foreign Office who could pass it on to the young queen but he got nowhere. He sent it to the Times newspaper instead where she might have read it over breakfast.

With diplomatic efforts failing to stop the trade, Lin besieged the British and other foreign merchants in their factories. He confiscated twenty thousand chests of opium and had them destroyed. This was greeted with outrage in Britain. The Duke of Wellington, the hero of Waterloo, declared that he had seen no insults and injuries as bad as those visited on the British at Canton. The Chinese deserved to be punished!

His views were echoed in an ever more jingoistic nation. Britain went to war. Even Tommy Staunton, the boy who'd charmed the emperor Qianlong on the Macartney expedition, who was now Sir George Thomas Staunton, a member of parliament representing Portsmouth, voted for conflict.

While many supported the war, some were bitterly opposed to it. Thomas Arnold, the headmaster at Rugby school, called it a national sin of the greatest possible magnitude. William Gladstone, later to become prime minister four times, declared: 'A war more unjust in its origins, ...a war more calculated to cover this country with permanent disgrace, I do not know and have not read of.' He later wrote in his diary: 'I am in dread of the judgment of God upon England for our national iniquity towards China.'

The Nemesis. The world's first iron warship. From an 1844 engraving by S. Bull.

3 The Devil Ship

The emperor and those surrounding the Dragon Throne didn't believe they could be defeated by barbarians from a small island on the other side of the world. The barbarians knew better.

The British Navy was the world's largest and most powerful. The Qing Dynasty's lumbering war junks, painted red and black with large goggle eyes, were little more than tubs, useless save in the smoothest waters. They were more of a coast guard than a navy. Even the best armed junk couldn't match the firepower of the smallest British ships.

A recent book by two Chinese academics comparing the effectiveness of the guns used by the two sides summed up the difference in a phrase which loses something in translation but amounts to: 'English ships powerful and cannon accurate, Qing ships weak and cannon useless.'[9]

It meant Britain had control of the seas and China was forced to fight a land war. This still didn't worry the mighty Qing empire. They had 800,000 men under arms. 200,000 Manchu Bannermen with 600,000 Han Chinese soldiers to back them up. How could a few thousand barbarians pose any threat? Once again, the invaders knew better.

They'd learned about the antiquated weaponry of the enemy from Lord Macartney when he'd visited China half a century before and their spies had continued to probe for weaknesses. In 1832, the British East India Company sent the merchant ship, Amherst, to scout the Chinese coast. Karl Gützlaff, a Prussian missionary on board, examined the defences at Wusong and wrote: 'If we had come here as enemies, the entire army's resistance would not have exceeded half an hour.' [10]

He wasn't far wrong. Most battles in the First Opium War began in the morning and were over by teatime. If the cannon aboard the Chinese junks were ineffective, those on land were even more useless. Many had been left on city walls exposed to the elements, causing the barrels to rust. Attempts had been made to replace them but the new guns were often worse than the old ones. Records show, for instance, that one senior officer ordered 40 new cannon a few years before the British invaded but during testing 10 of them exploded, killing one soldier and injuring two others.[11]

British superiority was clear right from the start. When the first part of the British expeditionary force arrived, it launched a combined naval and ground assault on Chusan and captured it in a day. The British soldiers also demonstrated their eagerness to murder, rape and loot. The India Gazette, an English language weekly newspaper, gave this vivid description of what occurred:

'A more complete pillage could not be conceived than took place. Every house was broken open, every drawer and box ransacked, the streets strewn with fragments of furniture, pictures, tables, chairs, grain of all sorts — the plunder ceased only when there was nothing left to take or destroy.'[12]

The worst of it happened after the soldiers started drinking the Chinese spirit known as Samshoo. One officer reported: 'Its effect on them was of the most dreadful nature. A man no sooner took a small quantity than he was ... committing the most horrible atrocities.'[13]

This was a pattern that was to be repeated throughout the conflict. When the full expeditionary force arrived, it sailed up the coast, sacking city after city, its soldiers looting, murdering and raping as they went. There was at least one occasion when the rape became almost organised with the pretty girls saved for the regular troops and the rest left for the Sepoys of the British Indian regiments.[14]

Whenever a battle was joined, whether it was on land or sea, the result never seemed to be in doubt. The 'water braves' who manned the war junks fought back in vain against the 'wooden walled fortresses' of the British navy. They showed great courage and remained at their posts, firing their antiquated cannon while everything around them was aflame, dousing themselves with water to withstand the heat and fighting to the death.

It didn't take long for the British to work out that the gunpowder the enemy used was placed in a red barrel next to each gun. They became adept at hitting these containers, killing the water-braves and setting the junks ablaze.

When the British confronted the enemy on land, whether it was the elite Manchu Bannerman or the Chinese soldiers of the Green Standard army, the outcome was the same. The defenders were equipped with weapons two centuries out of date and had no experience fighting a well armed adversary. They were more used to standing sentry in front of palaces, patrolling city streets, chasing bandits, helping collect taxes, or facing an enemy with weapons even more primitive than their own.

Chinese muskets had an effective range of 100 metres with a firing rate of 1-2 shots a minute. In comparison, the British had weapons with at least twice the killing range and double the firing rate. Every British soldier had a firearm while only half the Qing forces had any sort of gun. The rest relied on swords, knives, spears and bows and arrows.

There were those among the defenders who were too old to fight. In the first of two battles at Amoy, records indicate that of the nine soldiers killed, one of them, was 59 years of age, and two others were not far behind. This was when the average life expectancy in China was less than 40. In some cases, their guns were older than they were. There is one example of a musket still in use 166 years after it was first fired.[15]

While the Chinese outnumbered the invading army by forty to one on paper, when it came down to it, the opposing forces were often equally matched. The defenders had thousands of miles of coastline to patrol and were thinly stretched. The British were far more mobile, moved rapidly and could strike anywhere they wanted almost at will. It took them just 53 days to capture the four cities of Amoy, Dinghai, Zhenhai, and Ningbo. This was less time than it took the mandarin, Lin Zexu, to travel from Peking in the north of China to Canton on the south coast.

There were 12 battles during the First Opium War. The Qing army was only significantly larger than the British in two of them. In three engagements, the British had superior numbers.

Perhaps the best example of the gulf in technology and firepower between the two sides was the Nemesis, the world's first iron warship. She was armed to the teeth, nearly 200 feet in length and weighed more than six hundred tons but had a shallow draft of only six feet.

While Britain's wooden-walled men-o-war gave them command of the sea and major waterways, the Nemesis could navigate shallow waters and land troops close to battlements the guns of the British navy had already reduced to rubble. Powered by steam, she could tow warships reliant on the wind upriver on frustratingly still days.

The Nemesis had an immediate impact. The first time she saw action, her gunners fired a rocket at a large war junk. It struck the magazine and witnesses described how the Chinese vessel went up like a great firework. The smoke, flame, and thunder of the detonation left both sides gaping open-mouthed. The fragments raining down from heaven included the severed limbs and body parts of those on board. The Nemesis and her crew wreaked havoc that day. Shot from her 32 pounders was seen to go 'slap through one junk and into another'. After this encounter the British nicknamed her the 'Nevermiss'.[16] The Chinese had another name for her; they called her the Devil Ship.

The Qing tried to counter the threat of the Nemesis and other steamships by also building vessels that didn't rely on sail. Late in the war, they built 20 boats with paddlewheels for the defence of Zhenhai.[17] They weren't powered by steam. They relied on human muscle. It is unclear whether they were aping the British or copying an old Ming dynasty design used a few hundred years before. Wherever the idea came from it did no good. Zhenhai fell in a day.

The resistance was often fierce but hopeless. The captain of the Nemesis, William Hall wrote in his memoirs: 'Those of us who have witnessed the individual bravery, be it courage or despair, in almost every encounter will be slow to stamp them as cowardly people, however inefficient they may be as fighting men against European discipline and modern weapons.'[18]

There were generals who took their own lives rather than surrender. The commander at Amoy charged into the sea and straight toward the British fleet when he realised the battle was lost. For him, drowning was better than dishonour. The British killed hundreds that day for the loss of just two men. When it was clear the city of Zhenjiang was about to fall, the Manchu general made a pile of his papers, sat down on top of it, and set himself alight. He was so ashamed of failing his emperor.

Those who did survive rarely admitted their failure. They would send reports back to Peking claiming victory or vivid descriptions of heroic defeat. The emperor was told that the defence of Chusan in October 1841 lasted for six days. He was led to believe the defenders killed thousands of the enemy but were eventually overwhelmed by massively superior forces.

In British accounts, which are more believable, the whole affair was over in less than a day and only a few of their men were killed while thousands of Chinese soldiers were slaughtered.

The elite Manchu bannermen usually put up a brave fight but they seemed terrified of retribution. It was common after the invaders had taken a city for them to find the black and bloated corpses of Manchu women and children who'd been poisoned by their menfolk who'd then slit their own throats. Whole families, sometimes numbering up to twenty people, were found hanging from the rafters of their homes.

While there were many Han Chinese in the Green Standard Army who fought to the death, there were also those who would run as soon as the first shot was fired. The tactic of drafting poorly armed and half-starved troops from cities a thousand miles distant to defend a place they'd never heard of did little good. They weren't about to die for their Manchu overlords or strangers.

China was too hidebound and lost in ancient tradition to have any chance of winning. The decisions made by its generals often relied on the teachings of ancient philosophers and out of date military histories where the bravery of the soldiers was considered the decisive factor in victory.[19]

The ancient adage 'when two strong warriors meet, the brave one wins' was a common belief among politicians and generals. Tradition didn't consider the enemy's modern rifles or an iron steamship equipped with guns which could cut a man in half from a mile away.

Tactical decisions were sometimes made based on superstition. The most bizarre example is when the defenders launched the only counteroffensive of the war. It was a three-pronged attack to retake Ningbo, Zhenhai and Chusan. As part of the preparations, the commander Yi Jing went to a temple dedicated to the God of War to pray for victory. While there, he also sought a divination from the priests who told him: 'If men with the heads of tigers do not greet you, your security cannot be guaranteed.'

Three days later, reinforcements arrived wearing tiger skin hats. Yi Jing saw this as prophetic. Consequently, he planned his offensive for the Day of the Tiger and picked out a general born in the Year of the Tiger, for the assault on Ningbo.

Perhaps predictably, it was a disaster. Winter had not yet released its grip and days of rain had turned the roads into mud. Half the porters carrying the Qing army's weapons and supplies abandoned them. Local peasants stole most of their food. The tiger hatted fighters were slaughtered almost to a man. They assaulted Ningbo armed with only knives. They didn't speak the same dialect as Yi Jing and although they were all crack shots, they misinterpreted his commands and thought they'd been ordered to leave their muskets behind.

The British also had a very efficient network of spies. A simultaneous attack on Zhenhai that morning was repulsed after a warning from an informant.[20]

It wasn't until the British were at the gates of Nanking and preparing to attack the city that China was ready to sue for peace. After more than two years of war, costing thousands of lives and millions in silver, China caved in and agreed to all of Britain's demands.

The original design for a medal awarded to soldiers who'd taken part in the First Opium War. The image of the British lion trampling on the Chinese dragon was discarded as too insensitive.

4 A Close Run Thing

It could have been a very different story. The invaders might have had better weapons and no fear of the armies ranged against them but their real enemies were disease and heat. Dysentery, cholera and malaria took a dreadful toll on the aggressors. By the time the British reached Nanking and China was ready to capitulate, only a third of the men could stand. The rest were either dead or too sick to fight.

Cholera was the worst. Sometimes, it took only a few hours after the first symptoms showed for a man to die. It was a horror to watch. First came the diarrhoea and vomiting, then the face turned blue with the eyes becoming desperate and sunken; the patient would gasp for breath and moan in his cot as his body contorted in agonizing cramps before silence indicated he had perished.

It wasn't unusual for as many men to die from the heat as from wounds inflicted in battle. In the final engagement at Zhenjiang, the British lost 36 men but only half fell to enemy fire. The rest died from sunstroke. The troops weren't blessed with the silk or cotton robes which kept the Celestials comfortable and cool in the summer heat. Each man had a heavy uniform primarily made of wool buttoned up to the neck, wore stiff leather socks and a heavy shako sat upon his head. At Zhenjiang, the men were so parched for lack of water that they were reduced to drinking from irrigation ditches filled with rotting vegetation. The heat of the sun and the flames of the burning buildings were a more savage foe than the Chinese that day.

When China agreed to negotiate, it must have come as a relief to the British. They were spared another battle. They could have taken Nanking with their greater firepower but couldn't have held it. Their ships were swarming with rats and the sick outnumbered those able to fight by more than two to one. Even those deemed fit for duty looked like living skeletons.[21]

The treaty that brought an end to hostilities gave Britain Hong Kong and opened more ports for trade. China also had to pay 21 million silver dollars in reparations. It was the first of a series of 'unequal treaties' which signalled the beginning of China's Hundred Years of Humiliation.

Opium, the root cause of the war, was not mentioned in the treaty but almost as soon as the ink was dry, notices were nailed up in occupied territories proclaiming that opium was on sale again, very cheap, an opportunity not to be missed. The narcotic began to flood into the country in ever larger amounts.

The initial design for the medal handed out to the victorious soldiers shows the lion of Britain with its forepaws firmly planted on the back of the dragon of China. While this was an accurate interpretation of the conflict, it was considered too insensitive. It was scrapped in favour of a medal depicting some

British military equipment arranged underneath a palm tree. The Latin inscription on it translates as: 'They demanded peace by force of arms'.

A cartoon by the French satirist, Henri Daumier, from 18 61, showing China being forced to sign a treaty legalising the importation of opium.

5   Spoil

On March 3rd 1843, five wagons, each drawn by four horses and escorted by soldiers, arrived in front of the Mint in London. One of the boxes had broken open and people could see it contained unfamiliar silver coins. When it became known it was the first instalment of the reparations paid by China, the delighted crowd gave three cheers.[22]

The tons of silver and the other concessions agreed to in the Treaty of Nanking were never going to be enough. More than a decade later, the value of goods imported from China was nine times that of British exports to the Celestial Kingdom.[23] The only commodity that could fill this gap was opium.

Britain returned to China in 1856, with the French in tow, demanding more concessions, including the legalization of the drug that was wreaking havoc among Chinese people. This time, the excuse for war was the Qing authorities seizing a boat called the Arrow for smuggling salt. There was some fierce resistance and setbacks for the invaders in the early stages of this, the Second Opium War, but once the full expeditionary force arrived, the outcome was never in question.

Once again, Western technology was decisive. This time, the British were equipped with Armstrong guns capable of hitting targets up to five miles away. Some allied officers declared themselves ashamed to have come so far to fight such a wretched enemy.

Red is considered a lucky colour in China but one can imagine the defenders felt only dread when they saw the British marching towards them in their signature red coats. The ample red turbans worn by many of the Indian soldiers who made up a third of the British forces may well have had a similar effect on Chinese morale.

While looting was widespread during the First Opium War, it wasn't particularly organized. The British had sailed up the coast, ransacking cities and grabbing what they could. The Second Opium War is remembered for the systematic looting and destruction of the Emperor's Summer Palace.

Yuanmingyuan, the Garden of Perfect Brightness, was a large walled park and palace complex on the outskirts of Peking. Many people think the Forbidden City was the place of ceremony and ritual but until its destruction, it was from the Summer Palace that the Son of Heaven dictated imperial decrees and consulted with his advisors. It was also a place where he relaxed with his family.

The names of the temples, pagodas and palaces that once stood there hint at the harmony this small piece of paradise strived towards. The Terrace of the Peaceful View, the Pavilion of Quiet Joy, the Temple of Gracious Memory, the Springtime Lodge of Apricot Blossoms, and the Marble Pavilion in the Grove of White-Barked Pines are just a few examples.

Yuanmingyuan was an archive, museum, and treasure trove, where priceless objects from all over the empire (and beyond) had been collected and stored for hundreds of years. When the emperor Xianfeng, a pale shadow of the men who had reigned before him, fled as the invading French and British approached, the hundreds of Manchu Bannermen who had patrolled the walls went with him.

The few eunuchs left behind were helpless to stop the invaders from taking possession. The French got there first. The eunuchs did try to put up a fight. They barred the doors and stood behind them in a fear filled huddle, armed with rusty swords and garden tools. French soldiers climbed over the walls and made short work of them before opening the gates to their compatriots.

The French soldiers didn't begin looting at first. They were overawed by what they found and walked around in hushed silence as if they were in a museum.

'In order to describe it,' wrote Maurice d'Hérisson, an interpreter with the French army, 'I would need to dissolve all known precious stones in liquid gold and paint a picture with a diamond feather whose bristles contain all the fantasies of a poet of the East.'[24]

This reverence didn't last long. As soon as the first soldier put something in his pack, the rest followed suit and began ransacking the palaces and temples.

Amid raucous laughter, soldiers lit their pipes with manuscripts taken from the imperial library, dressed up in the emperor's clothes and smashed priceless porcelain and delicate jade bowls to smithereens just for the hell of it. Eyewitnesses later remembered silk tapestries torn down, Frenchmen using clubs to smash vases to atoms and the wanton destruction of what could not be carried away.

The British weren't happy the French had got there before them. The next day, they joined in. They weren't alone. The 3,000 Chinese servants in their baggage train swarmed over the walls to grab whatever they could.

The British had an established set of rules for looting and sharing the spoils. According to Maurice d'Hérrison: 'They arrived in squads, like gangs of workmen, carrying large sacks and commanded by noncommissioned officers, to haul away as much as possible.'[25]

The loot collected by the British was placed in piles in front of the Hall of Audience, where one of the officers acted as auctioneer with an upturned tea chest as a podium and a pistol butt for a gavel. It was reportedly a 'merry' affair, where priceless treasures were sold for a fraction of their value.

One officer, Charles Gordon, who became known as Chinese Gordon for his later exploits in helping the Celestial Kingdom crush the Taiping rebellion, bought the emperor's throne. He donated it to his regiment. It sits in the Royal Engineer's Museum in Kent where it is still labelled on its website as loot.

The auction raised £26,000. The money was divided up among the officers and men. First-class field officers, £60; second-class field officers, £50; chaplains, £40; lieutenants, £30; ensigns, £20; sergeants, £7 and 10 shillings.; privates, £5 and 13 shillings.[26] A tidy sum for even the lowliest soldier but only a fraction of the actual value of the items looted. Even taking inflation into account this amounted to only a few million pounds sterling today. Many of the items are now worth more than this on their own.

The only ones who didn't receive any of this cash bounty were the three generals, Hope Grant, Michel and Napier, who relinquished their portions to be shared among their men.

Not everything made its way to the auction. Officers and

men alike wrote that they had acquired just the right 'gift' for each family member, especially the female ones. The soldiers of the Indian regiments were seen carrying off precious gold ornaments, which somehow didn't go under the hammer.

Fortunes were made. Lieutenant Harris claimed he got his nickname, China Jim, because he looted more from the Summer Palace than anyone else. In his memoir, he recalled that among other things, he took a seal from the emperor's quarters and acquired several valuable antique watches of European manufacture.

Thomas Wade, who would later become Britain's minister to China and one of the country's leading sinologists, took time from stuffing valuable manuscripts into his rucksack to translate the label attached to one of the timepieces. He told the lieutenant that it had been presented to Emperor Qianlong by Macartney, more than half a century before. China Jim also made off with two solid gold pagodas worth about £22,000 which would translate into more than a million pounds today.

Lord Elgin, the British High Commissioner to China, reported back to his masters in London; 'The emperor's Summer Palace taken and sacked affording immense spoil. Emperor fled to Tartary.'[27]

When they'd finished looting, Lord Elgin ordered every building in the Summer Palace burned to the ground. This was in retaliation for the torture and in some instances, the death of members of the Anglo-French expedition that had gone to the Chinese under a flag of truce.

The French commander, General Montauban, was so appalled at the idea of destroying Yuanmingyuan that he refused to have anything to do with it. He and his men marched off and left the British to it. They didn't forget their loot, though. Three hundred wagons were needed to cart it away.

It took nearly 5,000 British soldiers two days to burn down and destroy the Summer Palace. In a letter to his mother,

Chinese Gordon wrote, 'You can scarcely imagine the beauty and magnificence of the places we burnt. It made one's heart sore to burn them.'[28] Another British officer spoke of the light being so subdued by the clouds of smoke that it seemed as though the sun was undergoing a prolonged eclipse, of the world being dark with shadow.

The emperor's brother, Prince Gong, broke down in tears when he saw the smoke rising from the burning buildings. The Times reported that this had a greater effect on him than any other event that had occurred during the war. The emperor, Xianfeng, is said to have spat blood on hearing of the destruction. He turned his face away from the world and sought comfort in his concubines and opium. He never returned to Peking and died within a year.

The destruction of Yuanmingyuan shocked the world. Victor Hugo, one of France's greatest men of letters, wrote: 'One day two bandits entered the Summer Palace. One plundered, the other burned. ......We Europeans are the civilized ones, and for us, the Chinese are the barbarians. This is what civilization has done to barbarism.' He went on to write that he hoped a day would come when France would 'return this booty to despoiled China'.[29]

That day has not yet come. The Chinese Museum at Fontainebleau has hundreds of items looted from the Summer Palace. And Victor Hugo's hands are not clean. A Chinese teacher who visited his former residence in Guernsey in 1989 found a note of Hugo's dated March 23, 1865, which indicated that he'd purchased a quantity of Chinese silk goods from English officers, which they had 'robbed' from the Garden of Perfect Brightness.[30]

Both Victor Hugo and Chinese Gordon show the strange morality of Europeans at the time. Gordon was a deeply religious man, renowned for his honesty and refusal to take a bribe. Yet, at the same time, he had no problem with looting. Victor Hugo, shocked at the destruction of the Summer Palace, felt no qualms at buying things pillaged from it by the men who'd burned it to the ground. Not only did he buy silk goods from British officers, he was an active bidder at auctions of loot held in Paris after the French army returned home.

The destruction of Yuanmingyuan should not have come as a great surprise. The British did not cover themselves in glory during the nineteenth century. The world is fortunate that the Taj Mahal in India still stands. In 1831, Lord William Bentinck, the newly appointed governor-general of Bengal, wanted to sell the marble of the mausoleum as scrap. He only abandoned the idea when advised that it might provoke a mass revolt among the local people.

The Taj Mahal is one of the most beautiful buildings in the world. It has been described as a teardrop on the face of eternity. If an educated British governor could consider pulling it down, what chance would the Garden of Perfect Brightness have? As one of the officers, Wolseley later recalled: 'When we first entered the gardens, they reminded one of those magic grounds described in fairy tales,' but we marched away: 'leaving them a dreary waste of ruined nothings.'[31]

And while it was James Bruce, 8th Earl of Elgin, who ordered the destruction of the Summer Palace, it wasn't the first time his family had been involved in controversy. His father, Thomas Bruce, the 7th Earl, removed the Elgin marbles from the Parthenon in Greece. They remain in England to this day.

While the 7th Earl may have paid for the antiquities he took from Greece it is less clear whether his successor put his hand in his pocket for the extensive collection of artefacts he brought back from China. During the sacking of the Summer Palace, he observed that while he: 'would like a great many things that the palace contains,' he was: 'not a thief.'[32] This begs the question of how he acquired so many valuable Chinese treasures. After his death, they were put up for auction. The 86 lots included porcelain, bronzes, lacquerware and jade. It is clear that some of the pieces originated from Yuanmingyuan.[33]

Looty, the Pekinese dog taken from the Summer Palace and presented to Queen Victoria.

6 Looty

One cannot move on from the sacking and destruction of the Summer Palace without mentioning the little Pekinese dog brought back to England by Captain John Dunne of the 99th Foot and presented to Queen Victoria and her husband, Prince Albert. According to Captain Dunne, the ladies on board the steamer on which he booked a passage home were so charmed by this tiny creature they fought for the privilege of taking it for walks around the deck.

If it charmed the ladies aboard the steamer, it had the same effect on everyone else when Captain Dunne stepped onto home soil with the dog. The Illustrated London News reported that it was considered by everyone who'd seen it as the smallest and by far the most beautiful little animal that had appeared in England.

Victoria and Albert had already received numerous gifts from the war, including a jewel encrusted silk tasselled cap and a jade covered book of the sayings of Confucius which had both been stolen from the emperor's bedroom but as dog lovers this gift delighted them.

It's sometimes said that it was Her Majesty who named her new pet Looty. This may or may not be true. It's more likely that some wit christened the dog with this name before it reached London but it gives an idea of how the sacking of the Summer Palace was seen by many as a thing of celebration and loot as the rightful spoils of war.

Looty's portrait was painted and exhibited at the Royal Academy. The little Pekinese also had many sittings with, William Bambridge, the Royal Photographer. The dog lived out the last eleven years of its life in luxury in the royal kennels.

Other Pekinese were also taken from the Summer Palace. They were not given to the monarch in what one supposes was an attempt to get into her good graces. They were looted, as was almost everything else, for profit. Captain (later admiral) Lord John Hay bred them at his family estate in Buckinghamshire and sold them at £50 each, which, taking inflation into account, amounts to thousands of pounds per puppy today.

The dogs have been a popular breed ever since. Two Pekinese puppies were presented to the future queen, Elizabeth and her sister Margaret in 1938. The gift was a feature in Country Life. Vanity Fair noted the little dogs were descendants of 'looted' stock. Every Pekinese in Britain is a reminder of the destruction of the Summer Palace, the Garden of Perfect Brightness.

A French cartoon depicting China as a pie being carved up by Britain, Germany, Russia, France and Japan. By Henry Meyer. 1898.

7   The Gayest Lark

Defeat in the Second Opium War forced China to open a further ten ports, expand Hong Kong's territory onto the mainland, and legalise opium imports. This was rank hypocrisy. In 1856, the same year Britain declared war, it banned the importation of the drug into its own country. The treaty that ended the war also allowed missionaries eager to save heathen souls to flood into every part of the Celestial Empire. They were given permission to build churches and preach anywhere they wanted.

Many Chinese people were already looking with a jaundiced eye at these barbarian priests. China had its own philosophies and religions dating back to before the New Testament. Daoist and Confucian temples could be found everywhere. Shrines dedicated to Buddhism were a common sight. Christian missionaries found stony ground in which to plant their faith.

There was a great deal of suspicion and resentment towards them. Some of this may well have been because of a bastardised form of Christianity introduced by a failed scholar, Hong Xiuquan, who believed he was the younger brother of Jesus Christ. Hong had fomented a rebellion between 1850 and 1864 that took more lives than the First World War. Some argue that the Taiping Rebellion, as it was known, had so distracted and weakened the Qing Empire that it could not effectively deal with the British and French forces that invaded and sacked the Summer Palace.

There was also the matter of opium. The Empress Dowager, Cixi, who was now ruler in all but name was well aware that force had been used to compel China to accept both the bible and the poppy. One of her advisors, Prince Gong, put it in a nutshell: 'Take away your missionaries and your opium and you would be welcome.'[34]

It wasn't just the bible thumpers who were resented. The merchants and engineers who came to make money at China's expense were no more popular. Western imports ruined many local industries and threatened millions with unemployment. This dislike of foreigners began to turn to hatred as the Western powers and an ever more aggressive Japan, began to scramble for a piece of the Chinese pie. In the last decade of the nineteenth century, Britain, France, Germany, Russia and Japan were all granted 'spheres of influence' while the empress dowager and her court stood by impotent to do anything about it.

A sore point was the railroads that were being built. The tracks ploughed through innumerable cemeteries and nothing was more sacred to the Chinese than the graves of their ancestors. Dark tales of human sacrifice circulated. The blood and body of a Chinese child were rumoured to reinforce every wooden sleeper under the railway tracks.

The situation was not helped by a series of floods and droughts that ruined crops and threatened famine. It was against this background that the hatred towards foreigners boiled over. There was a violent peasant uprising, usually referred to in the West as the Boxer Rebellion, to rid the country of the hated foreigners.

The rebels didn't call themselves Boxers. It was a name given to them by Westerners because of the martial arts they were seen to practice, which resembled boxing. They called themselves, *Yīhéquán*, which roughly translates as The Fists of Righteous Harmony. Many of them were fanatics who believed themselves impervious to bullets. This may have been the result of their somewhat chaotic leadership firing blanks at them to convince them enemy guns could do them no harm.

The Fists of Righteous Harmony believed that the foreigners swaggering around their country and the Chinese who'd converted to Christianity had knocked the world out of kilter. To restore order the land needed to be purged. They began by attacking Chinese Christians but as they grew bolder, they started to attack foreigners. The missionaries took the brunt of it. One Catholic bishop had his hands cut off. After lingering in agony for three days, he was doused with petrol and burnt alive. Hundreds of his converts were murdered.

Things began to spiral out of control when the German ambassador, Baron von Ketteler, was shot dead on the streets of Peking. The next day Empress Dowager Cixi declared that a state of war existed between the Qing and the foreign powers. She had chosen to throw in her lot with the rebels in the hope of driving out the hated foreigners once and for all.

Nearly 500 diplomats, missionaries and traders, their wives and children and an almost equal number of soldiers barricaded themselves inside Peking's foreign legations. They were joined by three times that number of Chinese Christians terrified for their lives. They were besieged by the Boxers and regular Chinese forces.

Armies from seven Western nations and Japan marched to their rescue. In a short, vicious, bloody war they lifted the siege. Then the murder, rape and looting began. The foreign armies stayed for months, committing atrocity after atrocity and plundering at will.

It's generally agreed that the worst offenders were the French, Russians and Japanese. Luella Miner, one of the American missionaries, had no doubt who was most to blame: 'The conduct of the Russian soldiers is atrocious, the French are not much better,' she said, 'and the Japanese are looting and burning without mercy.'[35]

George Lynch, the war correspondent for the Daily Mail, challenged the French commander, General Frey, about the behaviour of his men. The general's response was: 'It is impossible to restrain the gallantry of the French soldier.'

The French were held in low esteem by many among their allies. According to Henry Vaughan, the British officer in command of the 7th Rajputs, one of the British Indian regiments, they were the last to battle but the first to the loot: 'It is difficult to account for their absence on every important occasion,' he wrote.[36]

In the opinion of Gandahar Singh, who served with the 7th Rajputs under Vaughan, the worst offenders were Russian and French troops who would converge on a village, kill a handful of its inhabitants, strip the houses of all their valuables, bayonet the crying children, and then rape and kill the women.

Many thought the Russians were worse than the French.

One missionary bewailed the fact the women couldn't escape being raped because their poor deformed feet (as a result of footbinding) made flight impossible. Hundreds of women committed suicide to avoid being captured, abused and then murdered.

The new Summer Palace, which had been built at enormous expense to replace the one destroyed by the British forty years earlier, didn't escape. George Morrison, the correspondent for the London Times, cabled the paper to inform them that: 'The systematic denudation of the Summer Palace by the Russians has been completed. Every article of value is packed and labelled.'[37]

Gandahar Singh of the 7th Rajputs condemned the Japanese for their actions but praised them as the bravest of all the soldiers who'd taken part in lifting the siege. He admired their courage and damned their savagery in equal measure. He also recounted in his memoirs that: 'Japanese coolies, following in the rear of the army, decapitated aged men and women whom the troops had spared.'[38]

He also admitted that soldiers from the Indian regiments were not above looting and killing. They may have been less savage than some of their allies but they did their share. This is borne out by others. Bertram Lenox Simpson, a young ne'er do well who worked in the customs office, claimed he came across a whole company of savage-looking Indian troops molesting a group of female converts: 'green-white with fear, while a lady missionary vainly tried to beat them off with her umbrella'.[39]

The Germans, who didn't arrive until after the fighting was over, may have been latecomers to the party but they were among the most enthusiastic of looters. Count Alfred von Waldersee, the commander in chief of the Allied armies, made himself at home in the palace of the empress dowager, who'd fled the capital, and found a Chinese courtesan to warm his bed. Determined to obey the Kaiser's order that his men should behave:

'just as the Huns a thousand years ago', he set about plundering with methodical gusto.[40]

According to George Morrison, the count's men looted under the guise of important military operations even though the Chinese had been conquered before the Germans arrived. The Germans were nothing if not efficient. They made their prisoners dig their own graves and then shot them on the edge.

The British army was well versed in looting and had its own tried and tested methods of dividing up the plunder. Just as their predecessors had done when sacking the Summer Palace, they organised a Prize Committee and raised the money for it through public auctions of what had been collected by what they called authorised search parties.

The proceeds were then divided up based on rank and race. Indian soldiers were given one share less than British soldiers of equivalent rank, while native officers, regardless of rank, were given the same amount as British NCOs.

The medals handed out to those who helped relieve the Peking legations were stamped with the same design as that given to the soldiers who took part in the First and Second Opium Wars.

The reverse of each medal is stamped with the profile of Queen Victoria. She ages gracefully. In the one given out in the 1840s, she is a young woman; in the medal awarded 20 years later, she is a handsome, dignified, mature mother figure, and in the final version, she is a stern matriarch, the ruler of a nearly a quarter of the world.

In most accounts, the soldiers of the United States come out of this better than those of any of the other invading armies. Once the siege had been lifted, the city was divided up, with each foreign power being given responsibility for a sector. General Adna Chaffee, the American commander, banned looting in his zone. When a patrol caught two Indian soldiers from the 24th Punjabi Infantry in the act, they tried to arrest them. The Punjabis fled back to the British sector. Once on 'home territory', they began shooting at the Americans, who returned fire and killed them both.

The British were livid and to calm them down, General Chaffee ordered the two men of his patrol court-martialed. They were acquitted. To ensure the British knew where his sympathies lay, the general gave both men commendations for marksmanship.

It was well known among the Chinese that the soldiers of the United States were less savage than many of their allies. Within a month of the siege of the legations being lifted, Chinese people were flocking into the American sector, seeking refuge from the savagery of the other occupying forces. They came in such numbers that a housing shortage developed.

This doesn't mean to say the Americans didn't plunder but they did so with a certain wry humour. One shopkeeper begged an American soldier to write a sign to keep out looters. He obliged, scribbling: 'USA boys—plenty of whiskey and tobacco in here.'[41]

The Chinese residents of Peking were sorry to see them leave. In 1901, as they were making preparations to depart, a petition with thirteen thousand signatures was presented to General Chaffee, begging them to stay.

The American soldiers may have shown some restraint when it came to stealing Chinese treasures but the United States diplomats did not. Perhaps the man who stole the most was the Secretary to the American Legation, Herbert Squiers. He took home enough loot to fill several railway cars. He graciously decided to give some of it to the Metropolitan Museum in New York.

A reporter for the New York Times asked the Met how it felt about accepting loot. He was given a frosty reception. The curator, George H. Story, told him that The Metropolitan Museum did not accept loot. He went on to add: 'I think it an outrage, however, that such a suggestion should be made in connection with anything which Mr. Squiers has to give. ..... it would be presumed by the Museum that Mr. Squiers' collection had been honestly got, he being a gentleman without question.'[42]

Squiers made so much money from the treasures he'd either plundered himself or bought from other looters, he was set for life. Some of it went to purchase a 400-ton steam yacht. He christened her Invincible and moored her at Cowes on the English coast.

It wasn't just American diplomats who were guilty. Lady Ethel, wife of the British minister to China, Sir Claude Macdonald, was reported to have been at the head of one looting expedition. When the time came for her and her husband to depart Peking, she is said to have exclaimed, after having filled eighty-seven cases that she: 'had not begun to pack.' According to one British officer, she'd: 'devoted herself most earnestly to looting.' George Morrison wrote: 'All condemned the way Sir Claude and Lady MacDonald looted . . . 185 boxes at least.'[43]

Unrestrained theft by those outside the military probably reached a peak when the Forbidden City was opened to visitors. A contingent of British women headed by Lady Ethel visited the palace and observed Japanese soldiers cramming things into their haversacks.

The British women could not stand to see these things going to the Japanese soldiers so they helped themselves to several choice items. One cannot go without a souvenir they told themselves. The word 'souvenir' was used a lot. It sounded far better than 'loot'.

The Russians came out of the Forbidden City, their baggy trousers bulging with items they'd stolen. The American missionary, Luella Miner, observed that many: 'were more corpulent when they came out than when they went in.'[44]

The voices of the missionaries who might have been expected to protest were absent. In the words of the Daily Mail correspondent, George Lynch: 'They stood by silent spectators of this crucifixion of Christianity.' They didn't just stand by; many of them looted themselves.

Four American soldiers wrote about missionary looting to the Baltimore Sun. The soldiers admitted they'd done their share and would do it again if they had the chance, but they came down hard on the men of God: 'Speaking of looting, who did the most? The missionaries did the most of it,' they told the paper.'[45]

The missionary, Gilbert Reid, loaned the US Marines his English-speaking servant to assist them. While most of the missionaries who helped plunder Peking had the discretion to keep their mouths shut. Reid had no such qualms, telling anyone who would listen: 'I only regret I didn't have more time to loot.'[46]

This is from a man who later wrote an article called 'The Ethics of Loot' in which he claimed it not only harmed the victim but also those who did the looting. He argued that ethical standards should be upheld even in the chaos of war. The New York Evening Post was not impressed. It said of the article: 'It turns out on reading to be much loot and not much ethics.'[47]

Emma Martin, a young missionary doctor, helped herself to several items including a garment of taffeta silks, sandalwood fans, jade, a hair ornament, and embroidered shoes: 'I had just the best time ... it was such fine sport. I could hardly believe it was me. It was surely the gayest lark I ever had.'[48]

Those zealous to save souls seemed to have a strange moral outlook. Not all of them looted although a great many bought from those who did. Some tried to justify their behaviour by claiming the profits they made from selling plundered items went to help their converts, many of whom had lost their homes and livelihoods during the Boxer Rebellion.

Li Hongzhang, the Mandarin heading the negotiations that produced the Boxer Protocol that formally ended hostilities had little time for missionaries. He suggested that the eighth commandment should be amended to read: 'Thou shalt not steal, but thou mayst loot,'[49]

There were those who later seemed to understand they'd acted poorly. The missionary, Arthur Smith, who wrote a memoir of his experiences during the siege later helped persuade President Theodore Roosevelt that a substantial portion of the reparations paid by the Chinese to the United States should be used to found a Western style university in China.

The voices deploring the atrocities of the allied soldiers and the excesses of the civilians came from the journalists. They were not averse to looting themselves but they knew a good story when they saw one. Any report with the words loot or plunder made good copy. 'Civilization,' wrote the London *Daily Express*, should 'have the grace to blush'.[50]

The journalist who profited most was the correspondent for the London Times, George Morrison, an Australian by birth. Once the siege had been lifted, he made himself at home in the palace of a prince. He stole everything. As he candidly admitted: 'I have left him the glass in the windows, but nothing else'. He was so pleased with the riches he stole; that he named his new home Klondike.

Morrison wasn't the only Australian in Peking. A squad of fellow countrymen had arrived after the siege had been lifted. Their main task was to march prisoners of war to be executed. Like their more famous countryman, they did not leave empty handed.

People from more than 20 nations were in the Chinese capital at this time. In alphabetical order, they were American, Australian, Austrian, Belgian, Boer, Canadian, Danish, Dutch, English, French, Finnish, German, Hungarian, Irish, Italian, Japanese, Norwegian, Portuguese, Russian, Scots, Spanish, Swedish, Swiss and Welsh. Almost without exception, they would have returned home with some sort of loot.

Among the most successful looters were the Swiss hotelier, Auguste Chamot, and his American wife, Annie. They built a mansion on San Francisco Bay with some of the proceeds, decorating it with much of what they'd stolen. They also collected US$200,000 from the Chinese government as compensation for the loss of their hotel which had been destroyed in the fighting.

They were also shameless self publicists and liars. Auguste boasted he'd been wounded seven times and killed hundreds of Boxers. He told reporters that his wife Annie, one of only two women during the siege to use a rifle, shot 180.[51]

Their newfound wealth did not bring them happiness. They lost their mansion in the San Francisco earthquake of 1906. They divorced. Annie tied the knot with her chauffeur, a man thirteen years her junior. Auguste married a young manicurist named Betsy and drank himself to death. He gambled away his fortune and had only 15 cents in his pocket when he died in 1910. He was just 43 years old.

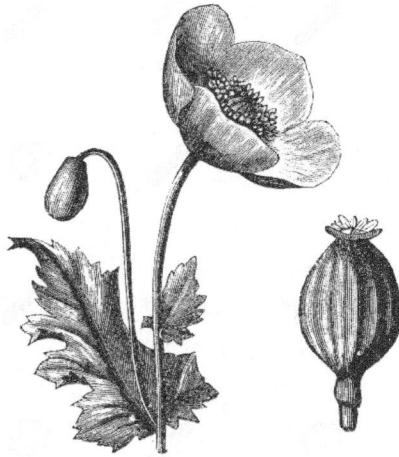

Papaver Somniferum, the Opium Poppy.

8 Opium

Opium is central to China's Century of Humiliation, and even in a book that focuses on the loot stolen by the West, it deserves a chapter. It is unlikely the treasures of the Celestial Kingdom would have been so thoroughly plundered if Britain hadn't needed to sell this narcotic to balance its books. Trafficking in opium robbed the Qing dynasty of the silver it earned through its exports and caused misery to millions of people through addiction.

While only 200 tons were being imported each year in the 1790s, this had risen to more than 2,000 tons on the eve of the First Opium War, and more than doubled to nearly 5,000 tons when imports were legalised in the 1860s after the Second Opium War.[52]

China's defeat in 1860 also paved the way for

missionaries, eager to save souls, to flood into the interior. They were shocked at what they found. On visits home to Europe and the United States, they reported on misery in village after village, of millions of lives ruined by addiction. They told those who would listen that a man would even sell his wife and daughters and plunder for the sake of it.

They complained that it was well known that the narcotic came from the same source as the missionary. The West had arrived with Opium in one hand, and the gospel of Jesus Christ in the other. It was impossible, they said, to teach lead us not into temptation and at the same time sell them a drug which was doomed to ruin them body and soul.'[53]

The voices of protest began to grow. In 1870, Sir Wilfred Lawson introduced a motion in the House of Commons condemning the opium trade but he was preaching to the wrong crowd. The Exchequer's income from it had grown from a pre-war one eighteenth to one seventh. His motion was soundly defeated.

Even William Gladstone, who thirty years earlier had bitterly opposed the First Opium War and railed against the pernicious effects of the poppy, now embraced the revenue it brought to Britain. It is perhaps ironic that Mr. Gladstone often drank an opium tincture, laudanum, to calm his nerves before giving a speech in the house.

In 1874, The Anglo-Oriental Society for the Suppression of the Opium Trade was formed. The dreadful effect of the drug on Chinese society could not be ignored it thundered but neither could the money it earned. By 1880, the British were shipping more than 6,000 tons of opium into China every year. While it was widely accepted that Britain had waged war to force the drug on the Chinese, its revenues were considered so vital to British interests that banning it would invite economic disaster.

Nevertheless, the tide of public opinion continued to turn. While the motion condemning the trade was roundly defeated in 1870, twenty-one years later, members of parliament supported a motion declaring that Indian opium revenue was 'morally indefensible'. Phrases such as 'England's Greatest National Sin' and England needing to 'Wash its hands clean of this foul iniquity' were being bandied about.

By the 1890s, China was consuming 85-95% of the global opium supply. The number of people who were slaves to the drug could be counted in the tens of millions.

It wasn't until Britain was no longer so reliant on the silver earned from opium and China began cultivating its own poppy fields that things began to change. By 1906, opium imports accounted for less than a tenth of what was being consumed in China. A year later, the British and Chinese governments negotiated a schedule of import reductions, but it was too late; the damage had been done.

According to the Chinese delegation to the International Opium Commission of Shanghai in 1909, opium consumption affected 23.3% of adult males and 3.5% of females. Although Britain as a supplier was now taking a back seat, opium was so much part of China, that the number of addicts continued to grow. The drug was so pervasive that it was offered along with wine to guests at weddings.

It wasn't long after this that the Qing dynasty collapsed. In 1912, a republic was formed. It soon foundered and China was carved up by warlords who often ruled areas larger than most European nations. These warlords encouraged the use of opium. Millions may have been addicted to the drug but the warlords relied on the taxes they levied on it to pay their men and buy weapons. It was also the only medicine readily available to their soldiers, who were legendary for the amount of opium they smoked. Many were addicts.

Even when Chiang Kai Shek began to restore some sort of order in the late 1920s, opium cultivation and use continued to thrive. Like the warlords, he needed its revenues to bankroll his regime and army.

By the late 1930s, some estimate that forty million Chinese people, 10 per cent of the population, were addicted. (Roughly equivalent to the population of England at the time). British-controlled Hong Kong had an even bigger problem, with an estimated 30 per cent of the colony's population dependent on it. Never before or since has the world known a drug problem of this scale or intensity.

Things didn't begin to change until the Communists came to power in 1949 and banned the cultivation, use, and sale of the narcotic. Dealers received the death sentence. Users were detoxed in hospitals, and those who relapsed were executed or sent to labour camps.

In 1960, the People's Republic of China declared with some justification that opium addiction had ended. In 1970, only one hundred tons of it was being produced each year for medicinal use.

This is not to say China is free of drug addicts but the problem is microscopic in comparison to what it once was. China can never forget that an addictive, illegal narcotic, was central to its Century of Humiliation. It is unlikely to let any drug take such a hold on the country again.

Wanrong, Last Empress of China. The photo was taken sometime between 1925-31 after she and her husband had been thrown out of the Forbidden City.

9 The Last Empress

Perhaps China's most famous drug addict was its last empress. Born into privilege, waited on hand and foot, and admired for her great beauty, she ended up a hollow eyed, stick thin figure who died from withdrawals, alone and forgotten on the cold stone floor of a prison cell before being thrown into an unmarked grave.

When she was a child, her family called her *zhilián*. There is no equivalent word in English. It means something like Lotus Plant but loses all its elegance in translation. She was given the name because she was fascinated by the lotus blossoms that floated on the lakes and ponds near her family home in Tianjin. She loved the scent of the flowers and would sit and watch them float on the water for hours at a time.

It was clear from a very early age that she would be a great beauty. She had the perfect teardrop shaped face and the soft almond shaped eyes so desired by Chinese men. When she reached her teens, she was told that she was to marry Puyi, the former emperor of China. The family packed their bags and moved to their mansion in Hatmakers Lane in the capital to prepare for this great honour.

As the wedding day approached, she would sometimes burst into tears. She was marrying someone she'd never met and moving to a palace cut off from the world to become wife to a man with no power and an empty title.

The Qing dynasty may have collapsed and the country may have been in chaos but the marriage went ahead with all the pomp and ceremony due to an imperial couple still ruling a great realm at the height of its power.

In the early hours of a chilly November morning in 1922, she left the family mansion, stepped into a sedan chair hung with imperial yellow brocade and roofed with a golden dragon to begin her journey to the Forbidden City.

The sedan chair was taken up by 22 noblemen who carried it with solemn dignity through the moonlit streets of Peking. It was preceded by gilded palanquins carrying the bride's ceremonial robes. A gaggle of eunuchs walked ahead and an army of princes mounted on fine horses cleared the way. Musicians, both Western and Chinese, filled the night with song. Blazing lanterns and fluttering pennants surrounded the cavalcade. Despite the fact it was winter and bitterly cold, tens of thousands of people turned out to watch what was to be the last imperial bridal procession in China.

She entered the Forbidden City where the noblemen carrying her sedan chair were replaced by eunuchs who set it down in front of the man she was about to marry. Throughout the ceremony, the bride wore a veil of crimson satin cloth embroidered with the dragon and phoenix. After she and Puyi had drunk wine from two goblets tied with silken thread, they entered the bridal chamber in the Palace of Earthly Tranquility.

She sat on the bed and with trembling hands, lifted her veil in anticipation of what might come next. The emperor, a boy the same age as his bride and with no sexual experience, fled back to his quarters in the Hall of Mental Cultivation. She was no longer little *zhílián*. She was now Wanrong Gobolu of the Manchu White Banner of the Eight Banners, Consort to Puyi, the Son of Heaven. Her loneliness had begun.[54]

She lived separately from her husband in the Palace of Gathered Elegance. She had her own chefs who would prepare anything she desired, including the Western dishes she was so fond of. She had her own tailor who sewed new clothes for her daily. Her maids dressed, undressed and bathed her. She was often seen by them admiring her naked reflection in the mirror. Not only did she have a face that could turn heads but also a figure that stirred the blood of men. All men, it seemed, except her husband.

She didn't like to eat alone and frequently shared her food with those who attended her. A servant, usually one of the eunuchs, was always on hand, so she had someone to talk to. When she did have visitors, she was reluctant to see them go. Sometimes, she made them stay until long after dark.

Wanrong had something of a temper. While she was usually considerate to her servants, she sometimes scolded them mercilessly. This often coincided with her periods. The imperial doctors were summoned and prescribed opium. No one thought anything of it at the time. Opium addiction may have been a huge problem in China but this was being given for medicinal reasons.

Her life in the Forbidden City didn't last long. In 1924, one of the warlords squabbling over the scraps of what had been the Qing empire marched into Peking with his troops and threw the emperor and his wife out onto the street. They fled to nearby

Tianjin, where they settled in the Japanese Quarter.

Wanrong was happier in Tianjin even though her husband kept a tight rein on her. He wouldn't let her dance the two-step, for example, as he thought it undignified. Her heart nearly broke when he cancelled a birthday party she'd organised for herself with a jazz band, dancing and a Western style buffet. Nevertheless, it was better than her isolation in the Forbidden City.

She was not always in the best of health. Perhaps some of this was due to her increasing use of opium, which she mixed with tobacco and smoked frequently. There were those, including her husband, who noticed she was consuming more and more. She knew he disapproved and said she would stop at once if it bothered him. Puyi did not insist.

Although it was the Japanese who had helped them after being evicted from the Forbidden City, she didn't like them. She knew her husband saw a chance to regain his throne through them but suspected they would only use him to legitimise their planned conquest of China. She warned him of this but he wouldn't listen. The emissaries from the Land of the Rising Sun began to see her as a threat. She knew that they spied on her. She began to hate them. They said nothing. They bided their time. They noted with interest her increasing use of opium.

In 1931, the Japanese seized Manchuria in northeast China and created the puppet state of Manchukuo. Wanrong's fears were realised when they invited Puyi to become its chief executive. When he agreed, she burst into tears and accused him of treason. He chose not to see that he would be no more than a figurehead in a puppet state ruled with an iron fist from Tokyo. Wanrong refused to go with him at first. She stayed behind in Tianjin but as a dutiful Chinese wife, she was soon persuaded to join him in his new capital, Changchun.

It wasn't long before Puyi was elevated from head of state to emperor. One of the last formal public appearances that Wanrong made was at his coronation in 1934, where she was declared Empress of Manchukuo. After this, she withdrew from the world. She started to have her meals brought up to her room. Her consumption of opium increased dramatically.

There were whispers of her having affairs with servants. Puyi returned from a trip to Japan to find she was pregnant. She gave birth to a baby girl, which Puyi knew couldn't be his. No one knows what happened to the infant. One account states that the Japanese army doctor who delivered the baby killed it by injection in front of her. Another story is that on the orders of her furious, cuckolded husband, the infant was thrown, still living, into a furnace.

After her baby was taken away, Wanrong began to neglect herself. She didn't bother to have her toenails cut and they began to grow inwards and bite into her flesh. She forgot to wash and started to smell. Her teeth blackened from constant smoking. She had no appetite and became stick thin. She had her hair cropped short because of lice so that it stood up in sharp spikes. Puyi was appalled at her physical deterioration. Her doting father stopped visiting her, unable to face what she'd become.

She was now smoking two ounces of opium a day, enough to kill an ordinary person. She hardly ever bothered to dress and spent her days poring over fashion and movie magazines. It's impossible to know how much she knew about what was going on around her. But she would undoubtedly have been aware of the escalating violence between Japanese and Chinese forces in the run up to the full blown conflict between the two nations, which began in 1937.

She did emerge from her stupor to condemn the marriage of her husband's younger brother to Hiro Saga, a member of the Japanese imperial family. She was still lucid enough to understand that Hiro Saga's son would be emperor if she and Puyi didn't have children. She was convinced this was part of a plot to get rid of her and refused to eat any food prepared by her sister-in-law in case it was poisoned.

With the outbreak of World War Two, the struggle between China and Japan became part of a larger conflict. How much Wanrong would have been aware of this is difficult to say. She was living in a dream world created by opium. She may not have known or even cared when the tide began to turn against the Japanese in 1944 and they started losing ground to Chinese and Allied forces.

It is likely she was shocked back to reality when the Soviets invaded Manchukuo in August of 1945. The Japanese army could do nothing to stop them. As the Russians approached the capital, Changchun, the imperial family fled. A train was arranged to take them to Mukden, from where they planned to fly to Korea and then to the safety of Japan.

They never made it to Mukden. Soviet bombing raids were so heavy the train was diverted to the small mining town of Dalizi. The imperial family, high ranking government officials, and the few servants and guards who remained loyal found sanctuary in a dilapidated two storey hostel. It was here that they learned atomic bombs had been dropped on Hiroshima and Nagasaki and that Japan had surrendered.

Puyi's Japanese minders told him a plane had been found to take him and seven others to Korea. He chose seven male companions, including his doctor and a servant but Wanrong and all the other women were left behind to fend for themselves. She wept as she was abandoned.

Puyi was aware that she was no longer capable of looking after herself. He asked Hiro Saga to care for her and make sure the former empress came to no harm. Hiro Saga promised she would do her best. This was even though, as a Japanese woman, she was in more danger than any of the other females of the imperial family who were being abandoned in the middle of nowhere by their menfolk.

Over the next few months, Wanrong and her party were betrayed, arrested and imprisoned, then released again. Wanrong's opium started to run out. She began to go into severe, life-threatening withdrawals. Hiro Saga used the group's dwindling funds to buy more. During the times they were locked in prison cells, she bribed guards to buy opium to feed her sister-in-law's addiction.[55]

They were imprisoned in the city of Jilin. There was little sympathy for the imperial refugees. In time, there was no more opium. Wanrong screamed for the drug but her pleas fell on deaf ears. She began to ache in every part of her body, her limbs spasmed uncontrollably, and she alternately burned with fever and shivered with the cold. She threw up until all that came out of her mouth was green bile. She writhed on the floor in agony, in a puddle of her own vomit, faeces and urine. Her mind broke. She mistook the guards for her maids and ordered them to draw her bath and prepare her food. They laughed at her.

They were not the only ones who found it funny. People came from miles around to watch this once beautiful empress grovel and beg for opium. There were others who were not so amused. Some of her fellow prisoners became so fed up with the noise she was making they begged the guards to put her out of her misery so they could get some sleep. The show only came to an end when bombing raids meant Jilin was no longer safe. Hiro Saga and Wanrong were loaded onto a cart and sent to a prison in Yanji.

Above the cart floated a banner which read 'Traitors from the Manchukuo Royal Family.' Wanrong lay in the cart and only occasionally opened her eyes to stare blankly at the hate filled faces that lined the road to jeer, spit and shout at them. She didn't seem to hear the curses thrown at her or bother wiping the spittle from her clothes.

The two women were separated when they reached their destination. If Hiro Saga stood on tiptoes and looked out of the tiny window of her cell, she could just see Wanrong's room on the other side of the courtyard. She'd fallen off her bed and lay unmoving in her underclothes on the hard concrete floor. Food provided by her guards had been left untouched for days.

Hiro Saga's pleas for someone to help her went unheeded. Her jailers told her Wanrong's cell stank to high heaven and they feared they would catch something if they went in to help her. One of them shrugged and said: 'Why bother? That one is not long for this world.'[56]

The Japanese princess did not give up. She had made a promise to Puyi that she would do all in her power to look after his wife. She persisted despite the fact she lived in terror of being executed. Eventually, she was permitted to go into Wanrong's cell, clean it and tend to the former empress.

She entered with a bowl of freshly cooked food she'd somehow persuaded the jailers to provide and tried to get her to eat. Wanrong didn't recognise her sister-in-law. She'd retreated from reality once again. She thought Hiro Saga was one of her maids:

'Are my clothes ready and is my bath drawn?' she asked.

'Yes, Your Highness,' replied Hiro Saga. 'It's time to get dressed; the emperor awaits you.'[57]

Lady Hiro Saga trembled as she looked at the frail woman who had lost touch with the real world. It had only been twenty-four years since a beautiful and innocent young girl had been carried by 22 noblemen in a sedan chair to be married to the last emperor of China. All that beauty and elegance was now gone, destroyed by the opium that had brought misery to millions of Chinese people.

Soon after this, all prisoners apart from the former empress were moved to another location. As they were loaded onto a cattle truck, Hiro Saga asked what would happen to Wanrong and received assurances that she would follow in a separate carriage once she had recovered her strength.

Wanrong never left Yanji. She died in her cell. No one knows the final resting place of Wanrong Gobulo of the Manchu White Banner of the Eight Banners, the Xuantong Empress,

Consort to Puyi, the Son of Heaven. She was thrown into an unmarked grave.

Tens of thousands had lined the streets of Peking to see her wedding procession make its journey to the Forbidden City. Perhaps equal numbers spat on her and cursed as she made her way in a cart to her prison cell in Yanji. No one was there to see her die or even record the date of her death.[58]

Cartoon in Punch, September 1894, showing Japan's victory over mighty China.

10   Humbled by Dwarves

While the West looted China in the nineteenth century, their sins paled compared to what Japan did in the twentieth. The Land of the Rising Sun had already humiliated China in the Sino-Japanese War of 1895 and indications of what was to come were plain for anyone to see.

After taking Port Arthur, Japanese soldiers had gone on an orgy of murder, mutilation and rape. They'd paraded in the streets with human heads held aloft on bayonets. The defenceless and unarmed inhabitants were butchered in their homes and their bodies unspeakably mutilated. Anyone thought to be a Chinese soldier was shot.

Ariga Nagao, an aide to the Japanese commander, Field Marshal Iwao Oyama, told reporters that his commanding officer regarded the slaughter as quite justified: 'We took a few hundred prisoners at Pyongyang and we found it very expensive and troublesome to feed and guard them. We are taking practically no prisoners here.'[59]

Perhaps they were aping the British. After the First Opium War, one staff officer, Armine Mountain, tried to justify all the killing that had taken place: 'The Slaughter of fugitives is unpleasant but we were such a handful in the face of so wide a country and so large a force that we should be swept away if we did not read the enemy a sharp lesson whenever we came into contact.[60]

And while the West's regard for the people of China became lower and lower, its respect for Japan grew year by year. It almost seemed that the Western powers could only accept the Japanese as equals once they had shown they could match them in killing and destruction.

To the Chinese, defeat by their neighbours, whom they had previously sneered at as a nation of dwarves, was a far greater humiliation than losing to the armies of the West. Kang Youwei, who was at the forefront of attempts by China to modernise, described the war as his country's greatest humiliation in more than two hundred years.

Worse was to come. During the Second Sino-Japanese War (1937-1945), Japan used civilians and prisoners of war as guinea pigs in experiments, including vivisection on live victims, testing biological weapons and exposing people to deadly diseases. Thousands died. The West cannot be freed from blame. After the Japanese surrender in 1945, the crimes were kept quiet in exchange for the data collected from these experiments.

Japan was also responsible for one of the most savage acts during the twentieth century. Hundreds of thousands of civilians and disarmed soldiers were murdered during 1937 and 1938 in what has become known as The Rape of Nanking. Soldiers went from house to house, murdering, raping and looting at will. Babies were bayoneted and thrown into pots of boiling water. Men were castrated with rusty knives, organs were carved out of living people and some were roasted alive over open fires. People were buried up to their waists and then torn apart by dogs. If no dogs were available, the victims would be run over by tanks or cut to pieces with swords. Others were saturated in acid and died in agony.

Thousands of women were raped every day. Wives, students, teachers, virgins, nuns, grandmothers, even children. If they caught a woman in the street, they would gang rape her in broad daylight. If any resisted, they were shot. Little girls were raped so brutally that many died. Some killed themselves. When soldiers found it difficult to pierce pre-teen girls, they slashed open their vaginas to make things easier for themselves. Many of the victims were slaughtered by the rapists when they had finished with them.

Additionally, during the Second Sino-Japanese War, thousands of Chinese women, known as 'comfort women', were forced to serve as sex slaves for Japanese soldiers.

The Japanese plundered everywhere they went. There are more than 1,000 museums in Japan and it is claimed that between them, they contain almost 2 million Chinese cultural relics. Hundreds of these relics are on display at the National Museum in Tokyo. There is little doubt that most of them were looted from China. Eleven of them are labelled as Japan's national treasures and 147 items are designated as important cultural property.[61]

There are some in Japan who urge the return of what was stolen but there doesn't seem to be the same groundswell of opinion as there is in Europe and North America to give back what was taken by force of arms.

A wedding photo of Chiang Kai Shek and his bride Soong Meiling. The Generalissimo is suspected of ordering the looting of the tombs of the Qing emperors at Malanyu. His wife was often seen wearing some of the looted treasures in the following years.

11   Eunuchs and Warlords

It was not only people from Japan and Western nations who plundered. Chinese looters also had their part to play. They were active during the First Opium War; they were there during the sacking of the Summer Palace and the Fists of Righteous Harmony, who'd surrounded the foreign legations in Peking in 1900, did their share before the siege was lifted. But it was after this, during the final years of the Qing Dynasty and the chaotic decades that followed, that Chinese people stole the most. Those closest to the imperial family were some of the worst offenders.

In 1921, for example, one of the imperial dowagers died. Almost as soon as she'd breathed her last, eunuchs in the Forbidden City began to fight over her jewellery. News of them trading punches while her body was still warm leaked out. The newspapers were full of it. The citizens of Peking were outraged. Those running the imperial household voiced their disapproval. According to Puyi's Scottish tutor, Reginald Johnston, it wasn't the thefts that disturbed them, that seemed to be taken for granted; it was the fighting over her property they found unseemly.

All imperial treasures seemed to be fair game. When Puyi married Wanrong in November 1922, thieves prised the priceless jades from her wedding crown and replaced them with green glass as she slept. Puyi knew that the eunuchs who served him were corrupt and the anger at their brazen thefts slowly grew.

When he could stand no more, he ordered an inventory of the imperial treasures to see what was left. This led to even more trouble. Before the inventory could begin, the lock to one of the imperial storerooms was smashed and a window in another was forced open. It seemed someone wanted to grab what they could while they still had the chance.

Then, on the night of June 27th 1923, only days after the inventory had begun, a fire broke out in the Palace of Established Happiness, where the main storerooms were located. Ancient scrolls, porcelain, paintings, art objects and so much else were destroyed in the fire. The press pointed the finger of blame at the eunuchs, whom they accused of committing arson in the hope of covering their tracks.

An indication of the value of what had been lost can be found in the melted gold scavenged from the site by a bullion dealer who paid a fortune for the privilege of doing so. He collected nearly a ton of the precious metal from the ruins.

Less than two weeks after the fire, Puyi threw the eunuchs out of the Forbidden City. They were ordered to gather in one of the palace courtyards where they were told their services were no longer required. More than a thousand of them were marched out of the gates by armed guards. Over the next few days, they were allowed back, in ones and twos, to collect their personal belongings but the ancient tradition of the imperial family being served by eunuchs was over.

Puyi had had enough. They'd become so brazen about their crimes that he could no longer turn a blind eye. According to Reginald Johnston, some had even opened curio shops within sight of the Forbidden City, where they sold the treasures they'd pilfered.[62]

So much jade was stolen that dozens of lapidaries worked night and day to regrind them to cater to foreign tastes. The best customers were from abroad. They were the ones with money. The most popular jade was known as 'American Green' as it was the colour that foreigners preferred.

Worse was to come. On Monday the 2nd of July 1928, the imperial tombs of the Qing dynasty at Malanyu in Hebei province were looted by the warlord Sun Dianying. He watched from his car as his men blew open the great stone doors that guarded the mausoleum of the empress dowager, Cixi. He knew it must be stuffed with treasure. Imperial funerals were notoriously lavish affairs and hers had been the most extravagant of all. According to the Qing archives, 2.7 million taels of silver, which is more than 13 tons, had been spent on providing her with a final resting place.

The thieves were not satisfied with taking just the priceless ornaments surrounding her coffin. No respect was given to the mummified corpse of a woman who had effectively ruled China for half a century. Her funeral robes, into which had been sewn thousands of pearls, rubies, sapphires, and emeralds, were ripped from her body. Jewels that had been sprinkled over her corpse were snatched by the handful. Her mouth was prised open to steal a legendary black pearl the size of a pigeon's egg, which lay upon her tongue. The thieves then threw her corpse onto the ground to get at the mattress of gold thread on which she'd been laid.

Her tomb was not the only one that was desecrated. The coffins of Qianlong, his empress and four concubines were forced open, their skeletons thrown to the floor and all the treasure taken.

It is unclear who ordered the tombs broken into. It's unlikely that Sun Dianying was working on his own. He was a gun for hire, a minor figure with only a few thousand troops under his command. Most fingers were pointed at the Generalissimo, Chiang Kai Shek, of the ruling Kuomintang (KMT), which that same year had established a national government, and had at least nominal control of the area where the looting occurred.

Puyi, was convinced Chiang Kai Shek was behind it. He demanded those responsible be punished but no one was arrested. If Puyi had any doubt about Chiang's complicity, this was soon dispelled when some of the loot found its way into the possession of the Generalissimo's new bride, Soong Meiling. Puyi wrote in his memoirs that the pearls from Cixi's phoenix crown became decorations for Meiling's shoes.[63]

As the years went by, Soong Meiling, or Madam Chiang as she became known, seemed to have an inexhaustible supply of fabulous jade ornaments and jewellery. Some of it she gave away as gifts. One of the recipients was Winifred, the wife of General Joe Stilwell, whom Washington had sent to act as the Generalissimo's chief of staff when American and Chinese troops joined forces during the Second World War to fight the Japanese.

Stilwell, known as Vinegar Joe because of his blunt way of speaking, had very little time for Chiang Kai Shek and didn't bother to hide his feelings.[64] Relations between the two men were strained. Madam Chiang, always the peacemaker, gave the general's wife, Winifred, gifts of jadeite to try to smooth things over. It is possible these gifts were looted treasure.

In 1943, Madam Chiang appeared before Congress to rally American support for China's war effort against the Japanese. Newsweek reported that her jewels were of priceless jade. It was rumoured at the time that one of the rings she wore once belonged to Cixi and the bangles on her wrists had been taken from the imperial tombs.

Chiang Kai Shek may have gone far beyond complicity in plundering the tombs of the Qing emperors. A British lawyer, O. M. Lewis, has written an exceptionally well researched book in which he offers persuasive evidence that the Generalissimo sold off most of the remaining imperial treasures.[65]

In 1931, after the Japanese seized Manchuria in northeast China, Chiang ordered the contents of the Forbidden City, which had been turned into a museum, packed into thousands of crates and sent to Shanghai for safekeeping. As fighting raged across China, the crates were constantly moved to keep them out of Japanese (and communist) hands.

From the time the imperial treasures were shipped out of Peking, Chiang had control of the crates in which they were packed. There's always been some controversy over their fate. The numbers have never added up. When he was defeated by the communists in 1949 and fled to Taiwan, he took thousands of these crates with him. The Generalissimo's diary entry for Saturday, January 8th 1949, described them as the cream of the collection.

The communists had taken possession of thousands more crates before Chiang could move them to Taiwan but there has always been some confusion about the numbers. Some believe that not all the crates have been accounted for. Mr. Lewis is not alone in his suspicions that Chiang sold imperial treasures. According to the historian Sterling Seagrave, there has always been: 'tantalising speculation' that many items were sold overseas. He also points out that the way in which the crates were shuffled around over the years makes it impossible to establish what or how much might have gone missing.[66]

Looting by Chinese people continues to this day. It now takes the form of graverobbing and stealing from archaeological sites. In September 2018, 140 people were arrested after tunnelling into 3000-year-old royal tombs at Yin Xu, a UNESCO World Heritage Site in Henan province. They included members of 14 different gangs and a local party secretary. They did little to hide their tracks and were caught after relics were found on sale just a stone's throw from the site.[67]

Most grave robbers are poor farmers and migrant workers equipped with picks and shovels. They take great risks in the hope of huge profits. Take the example of Yang Mingzhen from Baoling village in Shaanxi province. He was told by construction workers digging on his family's land that they'd stumbled across an ancient tomb. That night, along with his father and uncle, he went to see what he could steal. The tomb collapsed on top of them and all three lost their lives.[68]

There are also professionals who use everything from high-tech probes to traditional Feng Shui masters as they search for burial goods such as jade ornaments, bronze vessels and pottery figurines. In 2015, the police arrested 175 people and smashed a network spread across six provinces responsible for stealing and trafficking artefacts worth an estimated US$80 million.[69]

As long as there are collectors willing to pay a fortune and ask no questions, this problem will not go away. No one is going to risk jail or their life to loot a tomb if there is no market for what they dig up.

Sir Claude Macdonald, the British Minister to China during the Boxer Rebellion, was caricatured by Vanity Fair in October 1901. He and his wife, Lady Ethel, were known for the large amount of loot they 'acquired'.

12   The Problem

If you have read this far, you will have a pretty good idea of the extent to which China was looted during the nineteenth and twentieth centuries and may want to add your voice to the growing number of people who believe that any relic, artefact or treasure taken by force should now be given back.

This is not a simple thing to do. To begin with, no one really knows how much was taken. Wild figures are bandied about but none of them seem to have a basis in fact. A popular claim in the Chinese press is that 1.64 million looted treasures are held in 200 museums in 47 foreign countries.

The source for these figures is usually cited as a UNESCO study. There is no such study. UNESCO quote from a 2009 article by Ji Ling in the magazine Art, Antiquity and Law. There may well be that many Chinese relics in foreign museums. There may be many more but not all of them are loot. Many of them will have been acquired legally.

Nevertheless, there are those who think this number is far too low. In the same year that Ji Ling wrote his article, the Summer Palace's director, Chen Mingjie, claimed that 1.5 million antiquities had been looted from the Summer Palace alone and were in 2,000 museums worldwide, 10 times as many as previously suggested.

The way China's treasures were stolen is still a sore point in the People's Republic. When the then British prime minister, Tony Blair, visited China in 1998, a journalist asked how he could justify the British Museum's continued possession of 23,000 Chinese antiquities, implying they were all stolen, which they weren't. It was a question still being posed when one of his successors, David Cameron visited 15 years later.

Very little evidence points to what was looted during the First Opium War. It's hardly mentioned in any of the memoirs that the victorious British wrote on their return.

The Second Opium War is a different matter. There are dozens of eyewitness accounts of the sacking of the Summer Palace and it is possible to trace some of the items. Much of the plunder was put on display in towns and cities throughout Britain and France.

Some of the loot was put on show in Paris. The Illustrated London News reported it as 'French Spoils from China.' Most of it went to form the Chinese Museum at Fontainebleau, created by the French emperor's wife, Eugenie.

While the location of items such as these is clear, the whereabouts of much of the rest are lost in the mists of time. Thousands of pieces were sold at auctions in Paris and London after the victorious armies returned. While catalogues of some of these sales still exist, the records are incomplete. In addition, researchers have found that not all of the items sold in Paris were marked as coming from the Summer Palace. They were mixed in with other lots which confuses things further.[70]

More than 150 years have passed since these auctions took place. While it may be possible to track down who some of these items were sold to, it would be nearly impossible to establish who has them now and, in many cases, even more challenging to establish whether or not they came from the Summer Palace.

Between 1861 and 1867, more than 1,300 objects were offered in London at two auction houses, Phillips and Christie Manson & Woods. The porcelain, jade, lacquerware, enamels, and other treasures that were snapped up found their way into antique shops, private collections, and museums. Tracking these down would be at least as difficult.[71]

Similarly, although the British ordered all loot handed in while they were still ransacking the Summer Palace so that it could be auctioned and the proceeds divided up among the men, some of it never went under the hammer. Many items were kept as souvenirs and given as gifts to family members. Descendants of the original looters still hold some of these items but most have been lost or sold over time.

If the sacking of the Summer Palace remains the headline event, what happened in Peking in 1900 was probably worse. While the sacking of Yuanmingyuan occurred over a few days, the looting in and around the capital continued for months. The provenance of what was stolen is even more difficult to establish.

There were no triumphant displays of the plunder as there had been forty years earlier. Public opinion was beginning to frown on the practice of looting. It didn't stop it going on. There was money to be made but people were more cautious about explaining how they had acquired the 'souvenirs' they later offered for sale. Most of it was sold privately to dealers.

Will the whereabouts of the ten trunks of loot that were taken away by one Russian officer, tentatively identified as Lieutenant General Lineivitch, ever be established? Are some of the items he stole among the many Chinese treasures on display in the Hermitage Museum in St Petersburg? What about all the other Russian soldiers? What happened to what they stole?

What about the Indian regiments who bivouacked in the Temple of Heaven and sold their loot to all and sundry? Who were their customers and how much did they take home with them? There were also the Australian soldiers who, like the Germans, didn't turn up in time for the fighting but were enthusiastic looters after the event. Are there attics in Australia with hidden treasures? What happened to the items taken away by people from other Western nations which were not part of the Eight Nation Alliance? More than twenty nationalities were present in the Chinese capital at the time.

Even when provenance is certain, there is no international law which says things must be given back.[72] The problem is that while several treaties, conventions, and resolutions address this issue, there is no clear legal requirement to return any of the loot.

Even where there is a will to do so, some Western museums are prohibited from disposing of their collections. In France, for example, selling or removing any item is against the law. The British Museum Act of 1963 prevents it from doing the same.

Laws can be changed and there are precedents. In 1998, 44 countries signed the "Washington Principles", an agreement to return works stolen by the Nazis. Similar legislation could ensure the return of colonial-era artefacts.

There are signs that this might already be happening. In 2017, the president of France, Emmanuel Macron, commissioned a report which recommended the complete transfer of property to their countries of origin. In Germany, the Prussian Cultural Heritage Foundation, which oversees 27 German museums, has called for international guidelines to help museums identify and return colonial heritage.

Museums are aware that this is an increasingly sensitive issue. Many of them are now diligently researching where their collections came from. While there are curators who acknowledge the moral and ethical arguments for giving back looted articles, such a decision is above their pay grade. In the end, it will be a political decision made between governments.

Perhaps because of this, many museums are reluctant to respond to requests for information. Queries are answered slowly, if at all. The Metropolitan Museum in New York is a case in point. It has never replied to my inquiries about the hundreds of items donated by Herbert Squiers, which he'd acquired in 1900.

All this hampers various Chinese government initiatives to reclaim what was stolen.[73] These initiatives remind Chinese citizens that efforts are being made to get back what was taken but most of what has been returned is the result of 'soft power' and proxies.

The government backed multinational Poly Corporation, a well known front for the Red Army, has spent millions acquiring and buying back relics. It displays them in a museum on the ninth floor of its imposing headquarters in the Dongcheng district of the Chinese capital.

Poly Corp came to the attention of the wider world in the year 2000 when it paid US$4 million to purchase three bronze heads of a monkey, ox, and tiger that had once graced a zodiac fountain in the Summer Palace. The fountain originally had twelve heads, and each one sprayed water for two hours a day, and all of them sprayed in unison at noon. They were removed from the fountain in 1860. Poly Corp later purchased a fourth of the bronze heads, this time that of a pig, for nearly US$8 million. All have pride of place in its museum.

China's position as an economic powerhouse means that foreign multinationals hoping to boost sales in China are keen to ingratiate themselves with the powers that be. One example is the return in 2013 of two more bronze animal heads from the fountain.

They'd caused worldwide controversy in 2009 when they were offered for sale in Paris by the auction house Christie's. The winning bid came from a Chinese citizen who refused to pay, saying they should never have come up for sale. Four years later, the Pinault family, which owns the luxury retail group Kering, which boasts Gucci, Yves St. Laurent and Stella McCartney, among its brands, gave them to China.

'By returning these two marvels,' said Kering's chief executive, Francois-Henri Pinault. 'My family is loyal to its commitment to preserving national heritage and artistic creation,'.[74]

A cynic might point out that this was done to boost sales in a country which is a huge market for Western luxury goods. A cynic might also ask whether these items would have found their way back home if there were no customers for Kering's brands.

It should also be noted that Kering owns Christie's, which initially offered these two bronze sculptures for sale. It may only be a coincidence that Christie's became the first international fine-art auction house to receive a licence to operate independently in China that very same year.[75]

Seven of the 12 heads have now been returned through purchase or donation. The whereabouts of the other five are unknown. They may still be in private collections. If that is the case, they may never see the light of day. Very few items looted from China now come up for auction. The controversy surrounding any such sale makes sure of that. It makes it very difficult for researchers to locate stolen treasures.

It is not just the government and corporations in China that are campaigning for the return of looted items. Individual citizens are also doing their bit. At one end of the scale, there are people like Liu Yang, who used his meagre wages to travel the world searching for artefacts taken from the Summer Palace. He published his findings in a book, *Who Collects Yuanmingyuan,* which lists 800 pieces that he believes were once imperial property.[76]

At the other end of the scale are billionaires. In 2013, the property tycoon Huang Nubo visited KODE, the West Norway Museum of Decorative Art. He wept on seeing a collection of marble columns taken from the Summer Palace and told the museum director that they had no business being displayed in Norway. Mr. Huang later donated US$1.6 million to KODE, and it wasn't long before seven of the marble pillars were shipped back to China.

The museum may well have used some of the money they were given to improve their security. In 2010, thieves broke into KODE in what can only be described as a Mission Impossible style operation. They disconnected the alarms before entering through a glass ceiling, rappelling down into the museum, and taking 56 objects from its China Collection. Three years later, shortly before Mr. Huang came to visit, 22 additional objects were stolen, including vases, jades and imperial seals.

After the second burglary, authorities received a tip about an object stolen in the first break-in. They were told that it was on display at a Shanghai airport. Norwegian officials, wary of upsetting China, did nothing about it. Kenneth Didriksen, the head of Norway's art crime unit, said at the time: 'We don't want to insult anyone.'[77]

Norway is not the only country where museums have been targeted by burglars looking for Chinese artefacts. A string of thefts began with the Chinese Pavilion in Drottningholm Palace in Sweden. In England, the Oriental Museum at Durham University, the Fitzwilliam Museum in Cambridge, and the Museum of East Asian Art in Bath have all lost treasures. So has the Chinese Museum at Fontainebleau in France.

In almost every case, the items taken and the speed of the burglary indicated they were stolen to order. Some arrests were made but those convicted were never those who masterminded the crimes and those who were caught never revealed who had hired them.[78]

We may never find out who took these items. They may well be in private hands. Ancient Chinese jades are treasured by collectors all over the world. Many have been purchased at great cost and the buyers are not always aware they're stolen property. Even those who are aware of their provenance are reluctant to give them back.

It is not only Westerners who hold this point of view. In recent years, Chinese collectors have also bought items that were once taken as loot. They consider them to be their legitimate property. Liu Yang, who continues to campaign for the return of what was plundered, bewails the fact that most of them are unwilling to hand them over.

The largest collection of looted objects where provenance is beyond question is in the Chinese Museum at Fountainbleu. Hundreds of objects taken from Yuanmingyuan are on display. Porcelain, lacquer, jade, bronze, crystal, and gold can all be seen in custom made cabinets. Almost the entire contents of a Buddhist temple that once stood in the grounds of the Summer Palace, including two large bronze dragons, enamel altarpieces and silk tapestries, are on show.

They were presented to Napolean III and his wife, Empress Eugenie, by French officers returning from the Second Opium War. The Empress had rooms built to display them at Fontainebleau. Her 'Chinese Salon', which opened in 1863, showcased not only loot from the Summer Palace but also diplomatic gifts from the king of Siam and the emperor of Japan.

The main focus has always been the treasures taken from China. The museum is quite open about them being looted. The local tourist bureau almost seems to boast that the contents are plunder.

Other blatant examples of Chinese artefacts stolen by the West are those in military museums. For many years, they were displayed as loot and seen as trophies of war. In more recent times, the word loot has often disappeared from the labels that accompany them. In some cases, the word still appears but it's more likely to be an admission of how the piece was acquired, not as something to be proud of. One example of this is the Emperor's Throne, which is on display in the Royal Engineers Museum in the county of Kent in England.[79]

As already mentioned in Chapter 5, it was a gift to the regiment from its most famous son, Charles Gordon, who became known as Chinese Gordon for leading a group of mercenaries known as the Ever Victorious Army, which helped crush the Taiping Rebellion.

Search online for 'throne' in the database of the Royal Engineers Museum and it throws up 'A wooden throne …. looted by Major Gordon during the sacking of the Summer Palace in Pekin, 1860.' There can be no doubt as to its provenance or who was guilty of stealing it.

A devout Christian, Gordon appeared incorruptible. While leading the Victorious Army, he didn't steal his men's pay like many Chinese officers and had men under his command severely punished if they were caught looting. How is it that a deeply religious man like Gordon could, on the one hand, be so appalled by the idea of his men looting but, on the other hand, have no qualms about stealing a throne from the Summer Palace?

It may not be the only thing Gordon stole. A beautiful lotus shaped jade bowl sits on the throne, along with other items taken from Yuanmingyuan. It was donated by the family of another officer many years later but was originally a gift from Gordon. In addition, Gordon is known to have sent furs, jade, vases, and enamels home to his sisters and mother.

Recent research has revealed the throne he took may have been displayed wrongly for more than a century. James Scott, who previously worked as deputy curator for the museum, points out it was taken apart and packed in a crate, then put back together when it arrived in England. It is oblong in shape now but the original may have been square.[80]

There is no question that a gold ewer on display in Scotland was taken as loot. It was presented to James Hope Grant, who commanded the British forces that sacked the Summer Palace. He was a tall, spare man described as made of nothing but muscle and bone and admired by those he led for his ferocity in battle.

While this fearsome warrior relinquished his share of the money raised from looting the Summer Palace, this didn't mean he left empty handed. The officers and men under his command presented him with a gold ewer while they were still plundering Yuanmingyuan but before they burned it to the ground.

Hope Grant survived the wars he fought in and died in his bed in 1875 at the age of 66. Nine years later, his widow, Lady Elizabeth, donated the ewer to the Edinburgh Museum of Science and Art.

There are three inscriptions on the ewer. One inscription, in Chinese, is engraved on the base and tells of its weight, the purity of the gold and the year it was made (1852). The other two inscriptions are in English. One reads 'Taken from The Emperor of China's Palace. Yuen Mien Yuen', the other reads 'Presented to Lieut. General Sir Hope Grant, Knight Grand Cross of the Order of the Bath by the Officers of the Army in China, Pekin. October 1860'.

And if anyone still doubts its provenance, further evidence is written in a biography of the General, where he is quoted as saying, 'The prize committee secured a beautiful gold jug, from which the Emperor of China used to pour rose-water upon his delicate hands, and this they presented to me in a very handsome manner'.[81]

The ewer has been on display in Scotland for well over a century. It can now be seen at the National Museum of Scotland in Edinburgh in its 'World Cultures, Exploring East Asia' exhibition (level 5).

Many items held by museums in the West were probably looted but the evidence is less clear cut. An example is the Song of the Jade Bowl, a collection of three poems by the emperor Qianlong, etched onto ten dark green jade tablets decorated with dragons. It is now an exhibit in the Chester Beatty Library & Museum in Ireland's capital, Dublin.[82]

While it is unclear where Sir Alfred Chester Beatty, a mining magnate and avid collector, acquired it, circumstantial evidence points to it being stolen in 1900 by the British minister to China, Sir Claude Macdonald. Fifteen years after this, an exhibition catalogue for the Burlington Fine Arts Club listed it as his property.

The Chester Beatty Library and Museum has fifteen jade books in its collection. There is clearer evidence that another of them, a Buddhist Sutra, was also plundered from the Chinese capital. Page 82 of the same Burlington catalogue states that it was in the collection of Lady Sackville and had been taken from the private apartments of Empress Dowager Cixi after she'd fled the armies of the Eight Nation Alliance. The museum is currently trying to establish provenance for its collections and has discovered that Alfred Chester Beatty bought it from Lady Sackville in 1923.

It seems strange that a country such as Ireland, which suffered so much under British rule in the nineteenth century, should hang on to items looted from another country by the same imperial power that dealt with them so harshly.

The books and manuscripts stolen from China can be counted in the hundreds of thousands. If they were weighed, it would have to be in tons. Thomas Wade, the diplomat and sinologist, who was reported by the Illustrated London News to be 'saving' books for the British Museum during the sacking of the Summer Palace, retired after forty years of sterling service in China and, in 1886, donated thousands of volumes to Cambridge University. One wonders if any of them were stolen.

Between 1913 and 1923, Edmund Trelawny Backhouse, a strange and enigmatic fabulist who survived the siege of the foreign legations in 1900 later gave eight tons of Chinese manuscripts to the Bodleian Library at Oxford University. The Bodleian describes the donation as one of the finest and most generous gifts in its history. One has to ask, were they all legitimately purchased?

The Times Correspondent, George Morrison, owned one of the most extensive collections ever assembled. He sold them all to the son of a Japanese industrialist. It is the core of the Oriental Library in Tokyo. While Morrison had already purchased a large number of volumes before the sacking of Peking in 1900, one can't help wondering whether he managed to add to his library once the looting started. After all, he made himself at home in the palace of a prince and boasted that he'd stolen everything but the glass in the windows.

While many looted items ended up in museums and private collections, some are still held by descendants of those who stole them. The auctioneers, Bonhams, offered two imperial jade carvings in November 2012. They had been put up for sale by the descendants of Captain Arthur Forbes Robertson, an officer of the 67th Regiment of Foot who had 'removed' them from Yuanmingyuan. There is no doubt that he stole them. They came with a handwritten note to his mother stating they were taken from the Summer Palace. They were quickly withdrawn from sale after howls of protest from China.

Even when confronted with overwhelming evidence that artefacts held by museums were looted, there are still those opposed to giving them back. They argue that only Western museums have the resources and expertise to properly preserve and conserve cultural artefacts. They clearly haven't been to China, which is extremely proud of its culture and cares for its relics in museums as modern and sophisticated as those in the West.

The news in 2023 that thousands of objects had been stolen from the British museum by one of its employees was pounced on by Chinese state media. According to the Global Times, it revealed massive loopholes in the museum's management and security and 'the collapse of a long-standing and widely circulated claim that foreign cultural objects are better protected in the British Museum'.[83]

Museums claiming they need these treasures to provide a platform for educating the public about world cultures and history have a point, but why is it mainly museums in Western countries that possess extensive collections of relics from other nations?

The British Museum has storerooms crammed with millions of things which are not British. It could be argued that it is not a 'British' museum in the sense of reflecting British culture. It is British in the sense it represents the country's imperial past when it was convinced of its superiority and believed it had a mission to educate and civilise the world.

There are those who say that returning looted items would leave significant gaps in museum collections, leading to fewer visitors and reduced funding. This is hardly credible. Only a fraction of any museum collection is on display at any one time. The rest, rarely, if ever, sees the light of day. Such relics belong in museums in their own countries. Why should citizens from China have to travel to Europe or North America to examine treasures from their own past?

The idea of loaning them back to the country they were stolen from is sometimes suggested. This is not a solution. As far as China is concerned, a willingness to borrow items looted in the first place implies acceptance of foreign ownership. The increasingly vitriolic calls to return what was stolen have made this approach problematic.

Wán Bì Guī Zhào is an ancient Chinese idiom which translates as 'Return the Jade to the Kingdom of Zhao' but has come to mean to return something intact to its rightful owner.

13 A Solution

I suggest these stolen treasures be replaced with high quality reproductions and the originals be returned to their rightful owners. There are precedents for this. Scotland has led the way. The Kelvingrove Art Gallery and Museum in Glasgow used to display a Ghost Dance Shirt taken off a corpse after the massacre of Lakota tribespeople by US soldiers at Wounded Knee in 1890. Following discussions with representatives from the tribe, the shirt was returned to them and the museum accepted a reproduction in its place.[84]

If this can be done with one object, why not with others? What about the Hope Grant Ewer displayed in Scotland's National

Museum in Edinburgh? There are artisans in China who would consider it an honour to create a perfect replica in return for the original.

What about the Chinese Museum at Fontainebleau? It contains hundreds of exhibits France openly admits were stolen from the Summer Palace. Why not replace them with copies? It might be called the Chinese Museum but there are also treasures given to them by the king of Siam and the emperor of Japan on display. The French did not loot these; they were diplomatic gifts.

Among the sixty or so items from the king of Siam are replicas of royal objects, including a crown, palanquin, parasols, weapons, and jewellery. They are no less beautiful than the items stolen from China and I doubt for one second that visitors are aware or even care that they are not the originals.

At a recent national exhibition of jade carving, I cornered a few of the master carvers I knew. I conducted a straw poll to see if they would be willing to use their skills to make copies of significant jades looted from China and now held by Western museums. As examples, I mentioned the five jade books that make up The Song of the Jade Bowl and the dozens of jades in the Chinese Museum at Fontainebleau. They all said it would be an honour to do so but made it very clear that it could only be done with government approval. This is a very sensitive issue where feelings run high, and a great deal of thought would be needed before they could commit themselves to such a project. They are right. Even in the West, this can only happen with agreement at the highest level. In the end, it will be a political decision.

If such approval is forthcoming, then Chinese craftsmen are the ones with the expertise to carry out such work. The ancient arts such as jade carving, calligraphy and painting are treated with great respect in China. A recent jade symposium by modern masters, which I attended, and where I was privileged to exhibit some of my work, attracted a quarter of a million visitors in just one weekend.

My area of expertise is jade. And I am convinced that Western museums and private collections are already bloated with copies. One of my early mentors, Huang Hezhong, was very knowledgeable in the field of ancient jades and was often consulted by auctioneers and collectors. One day, he gave me a book which catalogued the annual sales of jade by the major auction houses in China. He cackled with glee as he pointed out copy after copy. In his opinion, eighty per cent were reproductions. This catalogue is updated every year and I have seen it on sale in at least two of China's national museums. There is no reason to doubt that the contents remain just as dubious every year.[85]

These reproductions are sometimes so good they are indistinguishable from the real thing without a detailed examination by an expert. The skill of the people who make them is stunning. As an example, I cite the craftsman, Yao Shuming, from Bengbu in Anhui province. In the late twentieth century, he took the art of reproducing ancient jades to such a level that most experts today can't tell they are fakes.

He is a legend in the world of jade. My favourite story about him is of the day in 1991 when he was arrested by police at Xiamen railway station as he was about to board a train home. In a routine search of his luggage, officers found what they thought were stolen cultural relics. Mr. Yao protested his innocence. They were replicas, he told them. One was a copy of a jade from the neolithic Hongshan culture and the other was a copy of a piece from the Han Dynasty of two thousand years ago.

An expert from Xiamen Museum came to assess the jades. After a careful examination, he stated they were authentic. He was taken to see Mr. Yao in his cell, where he demanded to know where the suspect had acquired these treasures. Had he robbed a tomb? Had he bought them on the black market? Was he part of some smuggling ring?

Mr. Yao thrust a name card into the museum expert's hand. Look, he told him, see what is written here, occupation jade carver, speciality: *fǎng gǔ* or ancient copies. The expert examined the jades again, this time more carefully. A long conversation between the two men followed. It ended with the expert offering to buy the two jades from Mr. Yao. He said he had friends in Taiwan who would be interested in reproductions such as these. Mr. Yao boarded a later train with more cash in his pocket and an order for more copies.

I was sceptical about what seemed to be no more than an urban myth until I interviewed Yao Shuming for a previous book. A long conversation with a very humble man convinced me the stories about him were true. Mr. Yao never sold his reproductions as the real thing but knows that some of his customers had no such scruples. He told me of one instance where he sold a customer a copy for US$1,000, who later resold it as an authentic relic for US$70,000. His work isn't perfect. Someone else who bought one of his pieces made the mistake of selling it to a senior party official who discovered the deception. The conman was jailed for four years.

During the 1990s, Bengbu wasn't well known outside China as a centre for reproductions but it was a magnet for a few ruthless merchants who sold them abroad as the real thing for a huge profit. The main customers were antique dealers in Taiwan, Hong Kong, Macao and Singapore. Dealers also came from North America and Europe, where an interest in Chinese antiquities remained strong.

Many craftsmen have followed in Mr. Yao's footsteps. Superb copies are still being made in Bengbu. Ironically, some of them are bought by Chinese museums because they don't have the originals to display.

One of the biggest workshops in Bengbu occupies a three-storey building. On the ground floor are about two dozen carvers. On the first floor, a dozen more sit in front of computers in a room full of reference books. It has the atmosphere of a library. These are the designers who make sure the patterns, whirls and swirls match those on jades from ancient tombs. On the third floor are those who age the jade to make it seem thousands of years old.

Similar industries supply reproductions of ancient bronzes, porcelain, lacquerware and almost every other ancient treasure produced in China's rich past. If it is possible to find a way to return looted relics and replace them with high quality replicas indistinguishable from the real thing, it will go a long way to resolving an issue that continues to sour relations between China and the West.

There are those who would be opposed to this approach. They would argue a copy loses the intangible aura and beauty of the original. People who hold this view often cite the twentieth century German philosopher, Walter Benjamin, who penned an essay in the 1930s where he stated that 'Even the most perfect reproduction of a work of art is lacking in one element: Its presence in time and space, its unique existence at the place where it happens to be.'[86]

This is utter guff. It's known that in the early twentieth century the West was flooded with copies, many of which found their way into museums. The Royal Ontario Museum in Toronto, Canada, is a good example. In 2015, two experts, one Canadian and the other Chinese, examined its 1400 jades. They found that among the collection were reproductions and that in other cases authentication was problematic. One high profile artefact was x-rayed and found to be four pieces of jade cobbled together, using copper plates and glue.[87] This aura that Walter Benjamin and his supporters talk about is never in the piece itself. It is always in the eye of the beholder.

Research suggests that a visitor to a museum spends, on average, between 15 and 30 seconds viewing any one item. Studies have also shown that visitors typically spend less than twenty minutes at an exhibition. They walk through it at a rate of 200 – 400 square feet a minute. They are not experts. It is unlikely their enjoyment will be lessened if some of the exhibits they are looking at are expertly made reproductions.[88]

Whether or not museums and collections in the West will be content to hand over artefacts and accept copies in their place remains open to question but there is definitely a movement growing to return looted items. In an article published in Town and Country, Emily Burack lists treasures, artefacts and relics that were returned in 2023. While the list is dominated by treasures that had been stolen from Jewish people by the Nazis in the twentieth century, she also includes objects that have been returned to more than twenty countries from museums and private collections in Europe and North America, many of which were looted during the colonial period.[89]

China is one of those countries. Two seventh century stone carvings which had been on loan to the Metropolitan Museum of Art were given back in a ceremony at the Chinese Consulate in New York. I wonder if the hundreds of items looted by Herbert Squiers, which he donated to the museum, were mentioned. It would have been nice to have been a fly on the wall during that conversation.

Whether such a conversation took place or not, the Met is now reviewing its collections for looted artefacts. 'As a pre-eminent voice in the global art community,' explained its director, Max Hollein, 'it is incumbent upon the Met to engage more intensively and proactively in examining certain areas of our collection.'

Emily Burack's list also includes fragments of the Parthenon in Greece returned by the Vatican and Austria. Will the British Museum follow suit and return the Elgin Marbles? It holds more than half of what remains of the sculptural decoration of the Parthenon.

It could take an act of parliament for this to happen but there have been rumblings in the press that there may now be the political will to give them back. If this does happen, it could open the floodgates for the return of everything acquired under dubious circumstances during the West's colonial period, not just those things that were looted.

One country that has had some success in reclaiming artefacts that were stolen is Nigeria. The ongoing campaign for the return of thousands of Benin Bronzes from museums throughout Europe and North America has garnered considerable publicity in recent years. Even the Archbishop of Canterbury has returned a bronze that one of his predecessors was given as a gift.

Cambridge University is another institution that has given one back. In a speech to the United Nations in May 2023, Sonita

Alleyne, Master of Jesus College, said, 'The tone has shifted and the implication is that the time of Africa bargaining for, begging for, and buying back its stolen loot is over. It expects its cultural property to be returned.' If this is true for the thousands of relics stolen from Nigeria, then it must be equally valid for the millions of artefacts taken from China.

I've discussed the issue of returning looted relics and artefacts with scores of Chinese people of different ages and from different walks of life. Almost without exception, they all believe that what was stolen should be returned. The majority agree that some sort of compensation should be offered to those museums which accepted items they didn't know were looted. At the same time, a significant minority disagreed with this view and felt anything stolen should be given back as a matter of course.

I belong to an informal group, which meets every month to discuss a variety of subjects, including philosophy, ethics and history. When I asked the group what they thought should be done to resolve this issue, the response was quite passionate. We usually meet for two hours and talk over tea. This discussion went on for much longer and continued through dinner.

People in China are very proud of their culture. They want the return of what was stolen, but they recognise it is a complex issue but those I asked were almost unanimous in their belief that the willingness of the rest of the world to agree was dependent on China's growing power.

Everyone I spoke to sees China's rise as a significant element in the equation. As one student studying mathematics at a university in Shanghai put it, 'The only way is to make our country strong enough so they cannot refuse to return our national treasures.'

Most people I spoke to were also quite happy that artefacts purchased by legitimate means should stay in foreign museums. Chinese people are proud of their culture and happy to share it with the world.

This is quite humbling for me. I am British. While we seem unwilling to return items we stole, we also seem reluctant to share our past. If it appears that a culturally and historically significant British work might be sold and end up in a foreign collection, there is an outcry and, an export ban is placed on it while we scurry around trying to find the money to save it from leaving our shores.[90]

If British reaction to the loss (through legal purchase) is so vehement, shouldn't British people consider how Chinese people feel about having millions of their treasures stolen at gunpoint? Resolving this problem can only be good for international relations.

James Hevia, an academic who has written extensively on the way China was treated in the past, has this to say on the matter: 'The failure to address the issue of loot will continue to haunt relations between the West and the former colonial world until contemporary nation-states find an equitable way to deal with the legitimate grievances stemming from past wars. This is no less an issue for postcolonial African and Asian nationalists today than it is for their counterparts in China.'[91]

There is an ancient Chinese saying the members of the discussion group I belong to reminded me of when I broached this subject with them. It is *wán bì guī zhào*. It translates as 'Return the Jade to the Kingdom of Zhao' but has come to mean to return something intact to its rightful owner. It is time for the West to return what was stolen.

The implications of such a gesture should not be underestimated. It would give China great 'Face'. Face is a complex concept. Put simply, when you give someone Face, you show them respect. It is a crucial element in Chinese society for maintaining good relations with others. Leaders in the West should take note. Returning was was taken would go a long way to improve relations with the People's Republic of China.

Selected Bibliography

I read a great many books and academic papers while researching *Spoil*. Many of them are listed below. My personal favourites were: the Pax Britannica Trilogy by Jan Morris, The Stone of Heaven by Levy and Scott-Clark and Julia Lovell's The Opium War. During my research, I took copious notes from many books and in an effort to avoid accidental plagiarism, I used an AI enhanced Plagiarism checker to scan my final draft. It gave me a clean bill of health. Apart from this, the only other time I made use of AI was to help me put together a survey asking students at three universities for their views on whether looted items should be returned For those who want to delve deeper into what was looted, who looted it, when it was looted and where it is now, any books written or edited by Professor Louise Tythacott are essential reading.

Aisin-Gioro Pu Yi. Emperor to Citizen. Foreign Language Press, Beijing, 1965.

Backhouse, Edmund. Decadence Mandchoue: The China Memoirs of Edward Trelawney Backhouse. Earnshaw Books. 2011.

Barrow, John. Travels in China. Cambridge University Press 2010 (first published 1804).

Bickers, Robert and Tiedemann, R. G. The Boxers, China, and the world. Rowman and Littlefield. 2007.

Bingham, John Elliot. Narrative of the Expedition to China. Henry Colburn. 1843.

Burack, Emily. Is 2023 the Year Looted Art Returns Home. Town and Country. October 2023.

Chen, Laurie. Article on Modern Tomb Raiders. South China Morning Post. 19 Sept. 2018.

Conn, Steven. Do Museums Still Need Objects? University of Pennsylvania Press. 2010.

Dale, Melissa S. Inside the World of the Eunuch. A Social History of the Emperor's Servants in Qing China. HKU press. 2018.

Dividing the Spoils. Henrietta Lidchi (editor), Stuart Allan (editor) Series: Studies in Imperialism, Manchester University Press, 2020.

Entract, J P. Looty. A Small Chinese Dog, belonging to Her Majesty. Journal of the Society for Army Historical Research. 1972.

Esherick, Joseph W. Lost Chance in China. The World War II Despatches of John S. Service. Random House. New York. 1974.

Evans, Laura. The Role of Artist-Made Reproductions in Restitution Cases: How Museums Can Benefit from the Return of Original Objects to Source Communities. Theory and Practice, vol 3. 2020

Fenby, Jonathan. Chiang Kai Shek and the China he Lost. The Free Press. 2005.

Forsyth, Angus and McElney, Brian, Jades from China, 1994, The Museum of East Asian Art.

French, Paul. Through the Looking Glass – Chinese Foreign Journalists from Opium Wars to Mao. Hong Kong University Press. 2009.

Gelber, Harry G. Opium, Soldiers and Evangelicals. Britain's 1840–42 War with China, and its Aftermath. Palgrave. 2004.

Hahn, Emily. Chiang Kai Shek – an unauthorized biography. Open Road Media. 2015.

Hall, Captain W H. and Bernard, W D. The Nemesis in China, comprising a history of the late war in that country with an account of the colony of Hong Kong. Henry Colburn. 1847.

Hanes III, W. and Travis, Frank Sanello. The Opium Wars: The Addiction of One Empire and the Corruption of Another. Sourcebooks. 2002.

Harrison, Henrietta. The Perils of Interpreting. Princeton University Press. 2021.

Hernon, Ian: Britain's forgotten Wars: colonial campaigns of the 19th century. The History Press. 2016

Hevia, James L. Loot's fate: the economy of plunder and the moral life of objects from the Summer Palace of the Emperor of China. History and Anthropology. 1994.

Hevia, James L. English Lessons. The Pedagogy of Imperialism in Nineteenth-Century China. Duke University Press. 2003.

Hill, Katrina. Collecting on Campaign. British Soldiers in China during the Opium Wars. Journal of the History of Collections. Vol 25. 2013.

Hill, Katrina. Yuanmingyuan Artefact Index. Website detailing hundreds of items looted from the summer palace In Chinese and English. https://www.yuanmingyuanartefactindex.org/jade

Howald, Christine and Saint-Raymond, Léa. Auction Sales from the Yuanmingyuan loot in Paris in the 1860s. Journal for Art Market Studies. 2018)

Johnston, Reginald F. Twilight in the Forbidden City. Victor Gollancz. 1934.

Keown-Boyd, Henry. The Fists of Righteous Harmony. A History of the Boxer Uprising in China in the Year 1900. Leo Cooper. 1991.

Langellier, John P. Uncle Sam's Little Wars. 1898-1902. Greenhill Books.

Lay, H. N. (Chinese Secretary to the Earl of Elgin's special mission to China) Note on the Opium Question. Printed by M. S. Rickelby, Walbrook, E.C. 1893.

Levy, Adrian and Scott-Clark, Cathy. The Stone of Heaven. The Secret History of Imperial Green Jade. Weidenfield and Nicolson. 2001.

Lewis, O.M. China's Art for Arms: Finding the Missing Imperial Treasures . High Tile Books Limited. 2016.

Liu. Yang, Who Collects Yuanmingyuan (Chinese Edition) 2013.

Lovell, Julia. The Opium War: Drugs, Dreams and the Making of China. Picador. 2011.

Lucas, Joseph. The story of our opium trade with China: (paper read in the Friends' Meeting House, Hitchin, in March, 1892): LSE Selected Pamphlets, 1894.

Macartney, J. China in worldwide treasure hunt for artefacts looted from Yuan Ming Yuan Palace. The Times. 20 October 2009.

Malone, Carroll Brown. History of the Peking Summer Palaces under the Ch'ing Dynasty. Paragon. 1966.

Mao Haijian. The Collapse of the Heavenly Dynasty: Reexamining the Opium Wars.

Marshall, Adrian G. Nemesis. The first iron warship and her world. NUS Press. 2016.

McLean, David. Surgeons of The Opium War, The Navy on the China Coast, 1840-42. The English Historical Review, Vol. 121, No.

491. 2006.

Meyer, Karl E. The Chinese Want Their Art Back. NY Times. June 20, 2015

Miner, Luella. China's Book of Martyrs (1903): A Record of Heroic Martyrdom and Marvelous Deliverances of Chinese Christians during the Summer of 1900. The Pilgrim Press. 1903.

Morris, Jan. Heaven's Command. Faber and Faber. 1973. This is the first in her Pax Brittanica trilogy which examines the rise and fall of the British Empire in the 19th and 20th centuries.

Paine, S. M. C. The Sino- Japanese War of 1894-1895 Perceptions, Power, and Primacy. Cambridge University Press. 2003.

Palmer, Alex W. The Great Chinese Art Heist. GQ Magazine. August 2018.

Phillips, Barnaby. Loot. Britain and the Benin Bronzes. Oneworld Publications. 2021.

Platt, Stephen R. Imperial Twilight. The Opium War and the End of China's Last Golden Age. Atlantic Books. 2018.

Preston, Diana. The Boxer Rebellion. The dramatic story of China's war on foreigners that shook the world in the summer of 1900. Walker & co. 2001.

Procter, Alice. The Whole Picture. The colonial story of art in our museums & why we need to talk about it. 2020. Cassell.

Ringmar, Eric. Liberal Barbarism. The European Destruction of the Palace of the Emperor of China. Palgrave Macmillan. 2013.

Roper, Hugh Trevor. The Hermit of Peking. The Hidden Life of Sir Edmund Backhouse. Macmillan. 1976.

Rudolph, Susanne Hoeber and Rudolph, Lloyd I. with Kanota, Mohan Singh. (editors). Reversing the Gaze. Amar Singh's Diary. A colonial subjects narrative of Imperial India. Oxford India Press. 2011.

Seagrave, Sterling. The Soong Dynasty. Harper and Row. 1985.

Seagrave, Sterling with the collaboration of Peggy Seagrave. Dragon Lady. The Life and Legend of the Last Empress of China. Alfred A. Knopf. 1992.

Serrell, Beverly.Paying Attention: The Duration and Allocation of Visitors' Time in Museum Exhibitions. Curator The Museum Journal 40(2):108 – 11. May 2010.

Shan, Patrick Fuliang. Yuan Shikai. A Reappraisal. UBC Press. 2018.

Stevens George B. and Fisher Markwick, W. The life, letters, and journals of the Rev. and Hon. Peter Parker, M.D. Congregational Sunday School Publishing Society. 1896.

Swinhoe, Robert. Narrative of the north China campaign of 1860. Smith, Elder and Co. 1861.

Taylor, Jay. The Generalissimo. Chiang Kai-shek and the Struggle for Modern China. The Belknap Press. 2009.

The AMOT Guide to Military Museums in the UK, 2010/11 edition: Army Museums Ogilby Trust.

Thomas, G. The Looting of Yuanming and the Translation of Chinese Art in Europe. Nineteenth-Century art worldwide: a journal of nineteenth-century visual culture. 2008. http://www.19thc-artworldwide.org/index.php/autumn08/93-the-looting-ofyuanming-and-the-translation-of-chinese-art-in-europe.

Thompson, Helen. What's Behind China's Professional Tomb Raiding Trend? The Smithsonian Magazine. August 2015.

Thompson, Larry Clinton. William Scott Ament and the Boxer Rebellion. Heroism, Hubris and the Ideal Missionary. McFarland & Company. 2009.

Thompson, Peter and Macklin, Robert. The Life and Adventures of Morrison of China. Allen and Unwin. 2004.

Tothill, Vanessa. East Asia collections in Scottish museums. National Museums Scotland. 2021.

Twitchett, Denis and Fairbank, John K. (editors) The Cambridge History of China, Late Ch'ing, 1800-1911, Part 1. Cambridge University Press. 2008.

Twitchett, Denis and Kwang Chingliu (editors) The Cambridge History of China, Late Ch'ing, 1800-1911, Part 2. Cambridge University Press. 2008.

Tythacott, Louise & Kostas Arvanitis (editors) Museums and Restitution. New Practices, New Approaches. Ashgate. 2014.

Tythacott, Louise & Panggah Ardiyansyah. (editor) Returning Southeast Asia's Past. NUS Press. 2021.

Tythacott, Louise. (editor) Collecting and Displaying China's "Summer Palace" in the West. Routledge. 2018.

Tythacott, Louise. Exhibiting and Auctioning Yuanmingyuan ("Summer Palace") Loot in 1860s and 1870s London: The Elgin and Negroni Collections. Journal for Art Market Studies. 2018.

Tythacott, Louise. Trophies of War: Representing 'Summer Palace' Loot in Military Museums in the UK. Museum & Society, 2016.

United Nations Office on Drugs and Crime's World Drug Report 2008.

Vaughan, H B. Lt Colonel of the 7th Rajputs. St George and the Chinese Dragon. Alexius Press. Originally published in 1902 by C Arthur Pearson.

Waley, Arthur. The Opium War Through Chinese Eyes. Routledge. 1958.

Ward Fay, Peter. The Opium War, 1840–1842: Barbarians in the Celestial Empire in the early part of the nineteenth century and the war by which they forced her gates ajar. University of North Carolina Press. 1975.

Wecker, Menachem. The Imitation Game. Washington Post. February 27, 2019.

Wilson, Andrew. The "Ever-Victorious Army" A History of the Chinese Campaign under Lt.-Col. C. G. Gordon, and of the Suppression of the Tai-ping Rebellion. William Blackwood and Sons. 1868.

Wolseley, G. Narrative of the War with China in 1860, Longman, Green, Longman and Roberts. 1862.

Wong, Young-tsu. The Imperial Garden Yuanmingyuan. A Paradise Lost. University of Hawaii Press. 2001.

Yoshiaki, Sato. 'Settled Completely and Finally': A Japanese Perspective on the Repatriation of Cultural Property. Journal of East Asia & International Law, vol. 10.

Zhang Jianxiong and Liu Hongliang. A comparison of Chinese and British navy cannon during the Opium Wars. Renmin Chubanshi. 2011.

About the Author

Andrew Shaw is a former BBC journalist who moved to China in 2008 to learn to carve jade. He has since become a master carver whose work sells around the world. He's won numerous gold medals in national and international exhibitions for his work. His first book, Jade Life, about the Chinese jade industry was critically acclaimed and sold worldwide. This is his second book. He is now working on a book that brings together myths, legends and stories about the Stone of Heaven.

www.jadefiend.com

3curzon@jadefiend.com

Notes

[1] Jonas Hanway, quoted in Mintz, Sydney W. The Changing roles of foods in the Study of Consumption. Ch. 13 of In Consumption and World Goods. Edited by John Brewer and Roy Porter. Routledge. 1994.

[2] Antman, Francisca M. For Want of a Cup: The Rise of Tea in England and the Impact of Water Quality on Mortality. The Review of Economics and Statistics. 2022.

[3] There have been various translations of the poem by Qianlong over the years. The text in Chinese can be found on The Chinese Literature Podcast, which also has its own translation into English.

[4] Hevia, James L. Cherishing Men from Afar. Qing Guest Ritual and the Macartney Embassy of 1793. Duke University Press. 1995.

[5] Anderson, Aneas. Narrative of the British Embassy to China in the Years 1792, 1793 and 1794. Edited by Frances Wood. Earnshaw Books.

[6] Macartney, quoted in Hevia, James L. Cherishing Men from Afar. Qing Guest Ritual and the Macartney Embassy of 1793. Duke University Press. 1995.

[7] At its peak, the British East India Company was the largest corporation in the world. It had a monopoly on the opium trade with China in the eighteenth century. It produced the drug in India and sold it to licensed merchants who shipped it to British warehouses in Canton. From there it was smuggled into the rest of China. It was a hugely profitable commodity and the company limited production to keep prices high. When the company lost its monopoly in 1834 other merchants scrambled to profit from the

drug. The amount of the poppy under cultivation increased dramatically, prices plummeted and more and more Chinese people became addicted.

[8] Lin Zexu, quoted in Gelber, Harry G. Opium, Soldiers and Evangelicals. Britain's 1840–42 War with China, and its Aftermath. Palgrave Macmillan. 2004.

[9] Zhang Jianxiong and Liu Hongliang. A comparison of Chinese and British navy cannon during the Opium Wars.

[10] Karl Gützlaff, quoted in Mao, Haijian. The Collapse of the Heavenly Dynasty Sanlianshudian.1995.

[11] Zhang Jianxiong and Liu Hongliang. A comparison of Chinese and British navy cannon during the Opium Wars. Renmin Chubanshi.2011.

[12] The India Gazette, quoted by French, Paul. Through the Looking Glass. China's Foreign Journalists from Opium Wars to Mao. Hong Kong University Press. 2009.

[13] Hernon Ian. Britain's Forgotten Wars. Colonial Campaigns of the 19th Century. The History Press. 2008.

[14] Lovell, Julia. The Opium War: Drugs, Dreams and the Making of China. Lovell cites two separate sources.

[15] Mao Haijian. The Collapse of the Heavenly Dynasty. Mao Haijian. The Collapse of the Heavenly Dynasty Sanlianshudian.1995

[16] Marshall, Adrian G. Nemesis. The first iron warship and her world. NUS Press. 2016.

[17] Mao Haijian The Collapse of the Heavenly Dynasty: Mao

Haijian. Sanlianshudian.1995.

[18] Hall, Captain W. H. and Bernard W. D. Henry Colburn. The Nemesis in China. 1847.

[19] Things may not have changed that much. According to a special report in the Economist published in 2023, some officers in the PLA are still better versed in cultural matters than things military. In 2018 the *PLA Daily*, the official military newspaper, accused some officers and soldiers of being too negligent, proud, scared or incompetent to fight. 'Some are quite accomplished in antiques, calligraphy and painting, but neglect the study of combat methods and tactics.' Page, Jeremy. Unknown Soldiers. The Economist. Nov 11th 2023.

[20] For detailed descriptions of the farcical counteroffensive you can read excellent accounts in Julia Lovell's The Opium War: Drugs, Dreams and the Making of China and Mao Haijian's The Collapse of the Heavenly Dynasty: Reexamining the Opium Wars.

[21] McLean, David. Surgeons of The Opium War: The Navy on the China Coast, 1840-42. The English Historical Review, Vol. 121, No. 491 (Apr., 2006), pp. 487-504

[22] Hernon Ian. Britain's Forgotten Wars. Colonial Campaigns of the 19th Century. The History Press. 2008.

[23] Brook Timothy and Wakabayashi, Bob Tadashi. Opium Regimes China, Britain, and Japan, 1839–1952. University of California Press.

[24] Maurice d'Hérisson, quoted in Ringmar, Eric Liberal Barbarism. The European Destruction of the Palace of the Emperor of China. Palgrave Macmillan 2013

[25] Maurice d'Hérisson, quoted in Hevia, James L. English Lessons.

The pedagogy of Imperialism in 19th century China. 2003. (Ch.4 Beijing 1860: Loot, Prize, and a Solemn Act of Retribution)

[26] Ibid.

[27] Illustrated London News 22nd December 1860

[28] Charles Gordon, quoted in Whitworth Porter, History of the Corps of Royal Engineers, Vol I, (Chatham: Institution of Royal Engineers, 1889. Quoted in Scott, James. Essay 'Chinese Gordon' and the Royal Engineers Museum. In Collecting and Displaying China's "Summer Palace" in the West Edited by Louise Tythacott. Routledge. 2018.

[29] Victor Hugo expressed these views in a letter to an English officer, Captain Butler, on the 25th of November 1861. An English translation of the letter can be found in, "The Sack of the Summer Palace," UNESCO Courier (November 1985)

[30] Young-tsu Wong, A Paradise Lost: The Imperial Garden Yuanming Yuan (Honolulu: University of Hawaii Press, 2001.

[31] Wolseley, G J Lieut. Col. Narrative of the China War. Longman, Green, Longman & Roberts. 1862. One of the many eye witness accounts of the looting and destruction of the Summer Palace.

[32] Swinhoe, Robert. Narrative of the North China Campaign: Smith, Elder and Co. 1861.

[33] Tythacott, Louise. Exhibiting and Auctioning Yuanmingyuan ("Summer Palace") Loot in 1860s and 1870s London. The Elgin and Negroni Collections. Journal for Art Market Studies 2018. Elgin's collection was listed first in the catalogue, as Lots 1-86, organised into a general section (Lots 1-14), followed by "Lacquer Work" (17-26), "Porcelain" (27-49), "Bronzes" (50- 62),

"Enamels" (63-68) and "Carvings in wood/jade etc" (69-86).

[34] Thompson, Larry Clinton. William Scott Ament and the Boxer Rebellion. Heroism, Hubris and the "Ideal Missionary" McFarland & Company. 2009.

[35] Ibid.

[36] Vaughan, H B. Lt Colonel of the 7th Rajputs. St George and the Chinese Dragon. Alexius Press. (Originally published in 1902 by C Arthur Pearson)

[37] Thompson, Peter and Macklin, Robert. The Life and Adventures of Morrison of China. Allen and Unwin. 2004.

[38] Yang, Anand A. An Indian Soldier's Account of China and the World in 1900–1901. In The Boxers, China, and the World edited by Robert Bickers and R. G. Tiedemann. Rowman and Littlefield. 2007. Also worth reading is Reversing the Gaze by Amar Singh for its account of how Indian soldiers were viewed by their white British counterparts.

[39] Preston, Diana. The Boxer Rebellion. The dramatic story of China's war on foreigners that shook the world in the summer of 1900. Walker & co. 2001.

[40] Thompson, Larry Clinton. William Scott Ament and the Boxer Rebellion. Heroism, Hubris and the "Ideal Missionary" McFarland & Company. 2009.

(Kaiser Wilhelm II made these remarks in what is now known as 'the Hun speech' to German troops in July 1900 as they were about to sail to China to lift the siege of the legations. He told them: 'If you come before the enemy, he will be defeated! No quarter will be given! Prisoners will not be taken! Whoever falls into your hands is forfeited! Just as a thousand years ago the Huns under their king <u>Etzel</u> made a name for themselves, one that even today makes them seem mighty in history and legend, so may the name Germany be affirmed by you in such a way in China that no Chinese will ever again dare to look cross-eyed at a German!

[41]Prince Gong, quoted in Thompson, Larry Clinton. William Scott Ament and the Boxer Rebellion. Heroism, Hubris and the "Ideal Missionary" McFarland & Company. 2009.

[42] Herbert Squiers, quoted in Seagrave, Sterling. Dragon Lady. The Life and Legend of the Last Empress of China. Alfred A. Knopf. 1992'

[43] George E Morrison worked as a correspondent for the London Times in China. He was there during the 55-day siege of the Boxer Uprising, witnessed the fall of the last Emperor and the birth of the Chinese Republic. Differing accounts of his life can be found in The Life and Adventures of Morrison of China by Peter Thompson and Robert Macklin and Through the Looking Glass – Chinese Foreign Journalists from Opium Wars to Mao by Paul French.

[44] Luella Miner, quoted in Thompson, Larry Clinton. William Scott Ament and the Boxer Rebellion. Heroism, Hubris and the "Ideal Missionary" McFarland & Company, 2009.

[45] Thompson, Larry Clinton. William Scott Ament and the Boxer Rebellion. Heroism, Hubris and the "Ideal Missionary" McFarland & Company, 2009.

[46] Gilbert Reid, quoted in Thompson, Larry Clinton. William Scott Ament and the Boxer Rebellion. Heroism, Hubris and the "Ideal Missionary" McFarland & Company, 2009.

[47] The New York Evening Post, quoted in Thompson, Larry Clinton. William Scott Ament and the Boxer Rebellion..

[48] Dr. Emma Martin, a young missionary doctor, quoted in Thompson, Larry Clinton. William Scott Ament and the Boxer Rebellion.

[49] Li Hongzhang, quoted in Thompson, Larry Clinton. William Scott Ament and the Boxer Rebellion.

[50] the London *Daily Express*, quoted in Hevia, James L. Looting and Its Discontents. Moral Discourse and the Plunder of Beijing, 1900–1901. Chapter 5 in The Boxers, China, and the world edited by Robert Bickers and R. G. Tiedemann. Rowman and Littlefield. 2007.

[51] New York Sun, January 2, 1901.

[52] A wealth of information can be found on this subject in various academic texts such as Opium Regimes, edited by Timothy Brook and Bob Tadashi Wakabayashi, Julia Lovell's, The Opium War and The Opium Wars: The Addiction of One Empire and the Corruption of Another by Hanes and Sanello, While the statistics they provide vary slightly they generally agree with each other. This book uses the figures provided by the UN Office on Drugs and Crime's World Drug Report (2008)

[53] Lucas, Joseph. The story of our opium trade with China: (papers read in the Friends' Meeting House, Hitchin, in March, 1892) LSE Selected Pamphlets.

[54] I have cobbled together the description of the ceremony from various sources, all of which differ slightly. They include Twilight in the Forbidden City, a memoir written by Puyi's tutor, Reginald Johnston, The Last Emperor by Edward Behr and Puyi's own autobiography.

[55] The Wandering Princess. The autobiography of Hiro Saga.

Beijing Literature and Art Publishing House. 1985 (originally published in 1959) most of the details in this book about Wanrong's final days come from Hiro Sagas autobiography.

[56] Ibid.

[57] Ibid.

[58] In 2006, half a century after she'd breathed her last, Wanrong's younger brother, Runqi, conducted a ritual burial for his sister at the Western Qing tombs. A photo he'd kept of her was buried there.

[59] Creelman. J. The Massacre at Port Arthur. The World (New York), 1894. Quoted in Paine, S. M. C. The Sino-Japanese War of 1894-1895 Perceptions, Power, and Primacy. Cambridge University Press. 2003.

[60] Armine Mountain, quoted in Marshall, Adrian G. Nemesis. The first iron warship and her world. NUS Press. 2016

[61] Xu, Jing. China Daily. Chinese relics are labeled as 'Japanese national treasures' in Tokyo Museum. August 2015.

[62] Johnston, Reginald F. Twilight in the Forbidden City. Victor Gollancz. 1934. Johnston was tutor to Puyi, the last emperor of China. All observations by him are from his autobiography.

[63] Emperor to Citizen: Autobiography of Aisin-Gioro Pu Yi. Beijing Foreign Languages Press: 1989

[64] There is a museum in Chongqing dedicated to Vinegar Joe Stillwell. It describes the general as 'a great friend' to China for his help in fighting the Japanese invaders during the Second World War. This might raise a few eyebrows in the West as Vinegar Joe was helping Chiang Kai Shek and the Kuomintang who were also

determined to crush Mao Zedong. His contempt for Chiang Kai Shek might explain this.

[65] Lewis, O M. China's Art for Arms: Finding the Missing Imperial Treasures. High Tile Books Limited.

[66] Seagrave, Sterling. The Soong Dynasty. Harper and Row.1985.

[67] Chen, Laurie, Laurie. Chinese Tomb Raiders. South China Morning Post. 19th September 2018.

[68] Qin, Amy. Tomb Robbing, Perilous but Alluring, Makes Comeback in China. New York Times. July 15, 2017.

[69] Ibid.

[70] Howald, Christine & Saint-Raymond, Léa. Tracing Dispersal: Auction Sales from the Yuanmingyuan loot in Paris in the 1860s. The Journal for Art Market Studies. 2018. Of 2,224 items sold between 1861 and 1869 at auctions in Paris only 463 items were clearly indicated as originating from the Yuanmingyuan – whereas the remaining 1,761 were merely "mostly" from the Summer Palace.

[71] Tythacott, Louise. Yuanmingyuan and its Objects. Chapter One in Collecting and Displaying China's "Summer Palace" in the West Edited by Louise Tythacott. Routledge. 2018.

[72] While there is no single international law that requires the return of items looted during war, there are some conventions, which include: The 1954 Hague Convention for the Protection of Cultural Property in the event of Armed Conflict. The UNIDROIT Convention of 1995, for the restitution or return of cultural objects that have been stolen or illegally exported from their country of origin. The UNESCO Convention of1970, which prohibits the illegal trade in cultural property and encourages its restitution

[73] Examples of state initiatives include the China Cultural Relics Recovery Fund which gives Chinese businesses making donations tax exemptions and the Cultural Relics Information Publishing Online Platform, launched in 2017 to provide evidence of lost or stolen relics. It gives the names, photos and ages of the relics, as well as the time and location of the disappearance of each item.

[74] Jones, Y T. Two bronze animal heads, stolen 153 years ago, returned to China. Reuters. Feb 2013.

[75] Kering owns both Christie's auction house and the fashion brand Yves St Laurent. The bronze rabbit and rat sculptures were part of Yves St Laurent's estate that Christie's offered for sale. An excellent account of this is included in an article written by Peter Neville-Hadley in the June 17th edition of the South China Morning Post entitled China's 'stolen' cultural relics: why the numbers just don't add up.

[76] Liu Yang. Who Collects Yuanmingyuan. Jincheng Press. 2013.

[77] Palmer, Alex W. The Great Chinese Art Heist. GQ Magazine. August 2018.

[78] The string of thefts of Chinese antiquities from museums across Europe has been widely reported. In addition to Alex Palmer's piece in GQ magazine, there is an earlier article written by Karl Meyer for the New York Times in June 2015 called The Chinese Want Their Art Back which is very informative and a little less speculative.

[79] Tythacott, Louise. Trophies of War: Representing 'Summer Palace' Loot in Military Museums in the UK. Museum & Society

[80] Scott, James. 'Chinese Gordon' and the Royal Engineers Museum. In Collecting and Displaying China's "Summer Palace"

in the West. Edited by Louise Tythacott. Routledge. 2018. (It is not the only throne from China held in a British museum. The V & A was given a cinnabar throne which once belonged to the emperor, Qianlong, by a British potato merchant who'd bought it at auction. The auction house had obtained it from the former Russian ambassador to China after he fled the Bolshevik Revolution of 1917).

[81] Knollys, Henry. Incidents in the China War of 1860 Compiled from the Private Journals of General Sir Hope Grant, G. C. B., Commander of the English Expeditionary Force. William Blackwood and Sons. 1875.

[82] The background to how the book The Song of the Jade Bowl came to be carved can be found in The Stone of Heaven written by Adrian Levy and Cathy Scott-Clark. In the opening chapter, they recount how in the year 1745 the emperor Qianlong rediscovered what many considered a legendary jade bowl. It was famous in the time of Kublai Khan and imposing enough to be noticed by Marco Polo on his visit to China. It also caught the eye of an Italian monk, Ordoric, half a century later. He described it as 'two paces high' and brimming with wine. When the Mongols were chased out of China in the 14th century it was lost to memory, that is until, Qianlong found it being used as a cooking pot in a Daoist temple. He wrote three poems in praise of it and all three were immortalized in The Song of the Jade Bowl. It is made up of ten dark-green jade tablets, decorated with five-clawed dragons.

[83] Global Times. August 2023

[84] Evans, Laura. The Role of Artist-Made Reproductions in Restitution Cases: How Museums Can Benefit from the Return of Original Objects to Source Communities. Theory and Practice, vol 3. 2020.

[85] Chinese Art Auction Records, edited by Xin Hong and published by Hunan Fine Arts.

[86] Benjamin, Walter. The Work of Art in the Age of Mechanical Reproduction. 1936.

[87] Chen, Shen and Gu Fang. Ancient Chinese Jades from the Royal Ontario Museum. Cultural Relics Press. 2016

[88] Serrell, Beverly. Paying Attention: The Duration and Allocation of Visitors' Time in Museum Exhibitions. Curator The Museum Journal. May 2010.

[89] Burack, Emily. Is 2023 the Year Looted Art Returns Home. Town and Country. October 2023. Ms. Burack lists Egypt, Iraq, Peru, Ethiopia, Libya, the Palestinian Authority, Cambodia, Burma, Yemen, Turkey, Greece, Mexico, Thailand, Ivory Coast, Colombia and Indonesia as some of the countries that have been given back relics held by museums and private collections in Europe and North America

[90] In Britain, all works that are over 50 years old or worth more than US$80,000 need an export licence. Most are waived through, but older or more valuable pieces are assessed at monthly meetings of a government committee made up of curators, dealers and art historians. If a work is judged to be of cultural and historic significance it is kept in Britain under an export ban while domestic institutions try to raise the funds to buy it. An example of this is the, The Archers, a painting by the eighteenth-century artist Joshua Reynolds. In 2013, the government imposed a temporary export ban on the painting which had to be extended several times before the National Gallery found the money to acquire it.

[91] Hevia, James L. English Lessons. The Pedagogy of Imperialism

in Nineteenth-Century China. Duke University Press. 2003.

Printed in Great Britain
by Amazon

38912851R00066